JEWISH AMERICANS

JEWISH AMERICANS:
THE IMMIGRANT EXPERIENCE

Hasia Diner

HUGH LAUTER LEVIN ASSOCIATES, INC.

Copyright © 2002
Hugh Lauter Levin Associates, Inc.
Series editor: Leslie Conron Carola
Series design: Ken Scaglia
Layout: Charles Schoenfeld
Production editor: Deborah Teipel Zindell
Printed in Hong Kong
ISBN 0-88363-129-6
http://www.HLLA.com
Distributed by Publishers Group West

CONTENTS

INTRODUCTION

Jews have given a great deal to their American home. Jews who emigrated to America to escape the limitations of Europe viewed the United States as a "goldene medine," a golden state. They talked about it, wrote about it, and sang about it as something like a new promised land that treated them as equals and made it possible for them to be whatever they wanted.

America kept its end of the bargain. While it was not a straight line or quick and easy path for Jewish immigrants to move into American society's cultural, educational, or political inner circles, they and, more important, their descendants, did indeed end up by the beginning of the twenty-first century as one of the most educated, highly represented, articulate, and affluent minority groups in America. Given in fact the number of Jewish college presidents, filmmakers, senators, novelists, professors, jurists, and physicians, many no longer think of them as a minority.

But they are. America is still a predominantly Christian society. Debates over the Christian content of American public life still rage, and Jews hold onto cultural practices and religious sentiments that differentiate them from the vast majority of Americans.

Opposite: Statue of Liberty Hanukkah Lamp. Maker: Manfred Anson. New Jersey, 1985. Brass, cast. 23 x 16 1/2 in. HUC Skirball Museum. Purchase with Project Americana funds provided by Peachy and Mark Levy. Much like the freedom Jews have long celebrated in America, the story of Hanukkah commemorates Jewish liberation from political oppression and religious persecution.

7

Ben Shahn. Albert Einstein with Other Immigrants. *1937–1938. Fresco. 12 × 45 ft. New York. Community Center, Jersey Homestead, Roosevelt, New Jersey. © Estate of Ben Shahn/VAGA.*

However much Jews differ from other Americans, America has offered them a vast array of choices to express themselves and to serve as citizens of their country. How have Jews served America? What did they give it in return for the opportunities it gave them? What difference did it make for America that in the nineteenth century European Jews cast their eyes westward across the Atlantic and decided to emigrate to the United States?

Pointing out what Jews have done for America in terms of politics, art, music, popular culture, science, and education does not mean that they did it alone or that they were somehow unique or better than others. In every enterprise of public life where Jews left their mark, they worked with other Americans from every religion and ethnic background to add to the quality of American life.

No area of American Jewish contribution to America demonstrates this better than that of liberal politics and the labor movement. Jews prodded America's conscience. They used their newspapers and magazines, their pulpits and ballot boxes to proclaim that America could not remain a land that divided its citizens by color. The Jewish contribution to the civil rights movement from the beginning of the twentieth century was one of alliance building. Jews saw the plight of African Americans and determined it was wrong for a democratic country to mete out its rewards and privileges on the basis of invidious distinctions. They decided that part of their mission was to press for change. From the Jewish presence in the founding of the National Association for the Advancement of Colored People in 1909 through the civil rights struggle of the 1960s when Rabbi Abraham Joshua Heschel walked with Martin Luther King from Selma to Montgomery, Jews played a role in making America live up to its own creed.

So too the efforts of Jewish labor leaders—David Dubinsky, Sidney Hillman, Bessie Abramowitz, Rose Schneiderman—who helped to bring a living wage to the American working class. They began by organizing their own trade, the garment industry, but they also participated in the broad-ranged attack on *laissez-faire* economics, which gave employers a free hand in how they dealt with their workers. Jews in the labor movement said that

New Year's Greeting. Early 20th century. Germany. Printed paper. 11 5/8 x 8 3/4 in. HUC Skirball Museum. Gift of Grace Cohen Grossman. Produced by a German shipping company, this card advertised its virtues for Jews considering overseas immigration. Most Jews came to the U.S. on such German lines.

Leonard Bernstein.

was wrong. Workers, like all human beings, were entitled to a fair wage, and to protection. Jews in the labor movement, both in and out of government, promoted Jewish ideals about human dignity.

From Louis Brandeis, the first Jew to sit on the United States Supreme Court, to Ruth Bader Ginsberg, who serves there now, American Jews have used the legal system to argue for the creation of a more humane society. The law, Brandeis argued over a century ago, existed to protect individuals from the unfettered hand of big business. The law, Ginsburg argues today, needs to ensure the equal rights of women, members of every minority group, and the accused.

American Jews, particularly since the end of World War II, have fueled the nation's culture of learning. On college and university campuses, Jewish professors in nearly every field of inquiry teach America's students. Jews pioneered in such new fields as psychology and anthropology in the latter years of the nineteenth century.

As early as the 1960s, when laws barring discrimination did not yet exist, over 12 percent of all professors and 20 percent of those in elite institutions were Jewish. In later decades, up to the present, the percentage increased. American Jews as academics publish in the country's scholarly journals and contribute to the corpus of its intellectual output. As scientists, historians, economists, literary critics, sociologists, anthropologists, and indeed scholars in nearly every field, they have contributed mightily to the "life of the mind" of America.

So, too, in medicine, individual Jews helped bring American medicine to its world renowned state. The names of these Jews are legion: Morris Fishbein edited the *Journal of the American Medical Association* for a quarter century and reported in its pages the many innovations of the field. Joseph Goldberger and Joseph Rosenau helped create the field of preventive medicine. Goldberger helped eradicate the scourge of pellagra, while Rosenau wrote the long authoritative *Preventive Medicine and Hygiene*, which became in the early decades of the twentieth century *the* guide book for physicians and health workers. Bela Schick at Mt. Sinai Hospital in New York developed the test for diphtheria, Frances Pascher pioneered in the diagnosis of lupus, and Nobel Prize–winner Rosalyn Yalow developed a technique for measuring substances in blood. The names go on, with the two Jewish polio

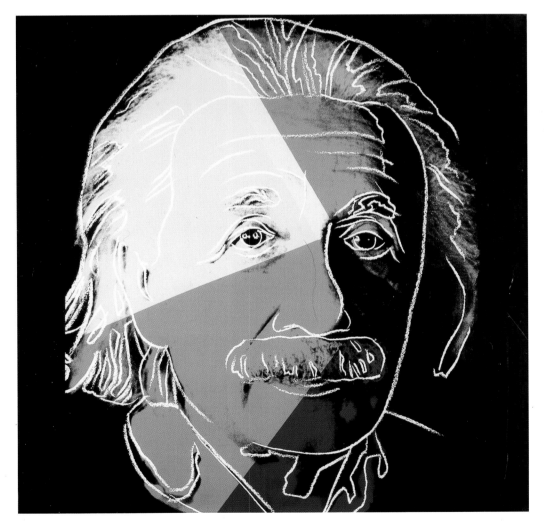

Andy Warhol. Ten Portraits of Jews of the 20th Century. *Albert Einstein. 1980. One from a portfolio of ten screenprints and colophon. 40 x 32 in. The Andy Warhol Foundation, Inc./Art Resource, New York. © 2001 Andy Warhol Foundation for the Visual Arts/ARS, New York.*

researchers Jonas Salk and Albert Sabin well known around the world.

The history of the Jewish contribution to the American mental health professions is an even more dramatic story. One estimate claims that nearly 50 percent of all psychologists and psychiatrists in American cities are Jewish, and whatever their therapeutic approach, they are all legatees of the work of the late-nineteenth-century Jewish physician in Vienna, Sigmund Freud.

Every area of mental health has had a large Jewish presence. Without Jews, American psychiatry would not have had the contributions of Aron Rosanoff, Laurtetta Bender, Leo Kanner, David Levy, Nathan Ackerman, Milton Rosenbaum, Daniel Offer, Nathan Kline, and probably most popularly known, Robert J. Lifton, who has written extensively on victimhood. In psychology the list is just as long, but we might mention Kurt Lewin, Charlotte Buhler, Heinze Werner, Arnold Lazarus, Marvin Goldfield, Edward Shneidman, and Abraham Maslow, a pioneer in creating the field of existential psychotherapy.

Freud once wrote, "Because I was a Jew I found myself free of many prejudices which restrict others in the use of the intellect; as a Jew I was prepared to be in the opposition and renounce agreement with the compact majority." Perhaps his words help us also explain the extraordinary Jewish contribution to American music, dance, film, literature, comedy, poetry, and theater—nearly every area in which creativity has been unleashed and creators have been unafraid to say, write, paint, or compose what they felt.

Spanning the cultural scene from the serious literature of Saul Bellow and Bernard Malamud to the "shtick" of vaudeville and the gags of stand-up comedy, from the twentieth century's vast output of Hollywood to the intense musical genius of Aaron Copland and Leonard Bernstein, from the songs written on Tin Pan Alley to those heard on Broadway, American Jews felt that they could express themselves as they wanted. They helped create American popular culture. The movies, comic books, television shows, novels, and plays that have been broadly disseminated in America and beyond have been in part the products of the Jewish people in America. Television,

radio, film, live theater, books, newspapers and magazines offered Jews a chance to explore their ideas about America and the human condition. The roster of names of Jews in the realm of cultural production is just too long to enumerate. The length would, however, be evidence of the enormity of their productivity and the perfect fit between America and the Jews.

No governments, no established churches, no encrusted elites kept them out. No laws could hold them back. Where opportunities existed, they took them. Where no opportunities were present, they created new ones.

Jews were not alone in shaping American culture and in redefining the nature of American political life. It was not Jews alone who taught, healed, and entertained, who made America a more humane society. But America would surely have been a poorer place, in body, mind, and spirit, had Jews not made the journey to this, their golden land.

Ticket line in front of the St. James Theatre in New York, April 2001, for Mel Brooks's Broadway production of The Producers, *based on his 1968 film. Mel Brooks won an Academy Award for his work on the original film, an early and daring treatment of the Holocaust in American popular culture.*

Larry Rivers. History of Matzah, The Story of the Jews (Part I—Before the Diaspora). *1982. Acrylic on canvas.*
116 3/4 x 166 1/2 in. Private collection, New York. © Larry Rivers/Licensed by VAGA, New York, NY.

THE WORLD AND THE JEWS

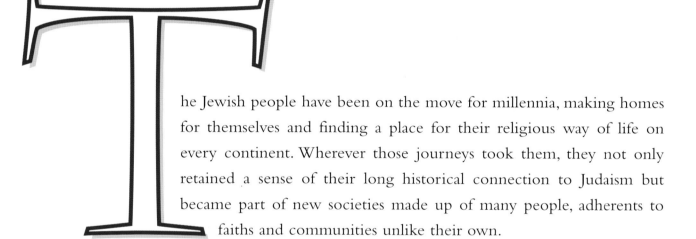

The Jewish people have been on the move for millennia, making homes for themselves and finding a place for their religious way of life on every continent. Wherever those journeys took them, they not only retained a sense of their long historical connection to Judaism but became part of new societies made up of many people, adherents to faiths and communities unlike their own.

Born in the Near East, the forerunners of America's Jews were nurtured in a land their holy texts had promised to them, a place known by various names—Canaan, Israel, Judea, Palestine. In that strip of land midway between Egypt and the Fertile Crescent, they established their identity, institutions, and sacred system, based fundamentally on the principle of monotheism, the idea that there was only one God, whose word had been revealed to Moses as law.

Wherever the Jews lived, they turned to that promised place when they prayed, and they expressed a vision that someday they would return there. Most never did. They found new places to construct their homes and communities, and the idea of returning to that land existed primarily on a spiritual and rhetorical level.

Their history was one of movement and change, and their religious system evolved in response to new circumstances. Over time the Bible was joined as a sacred text by the Talmud, the oral law, codified by rabbis who created guidelines for the day-to-day workings of Judaic civilization.

New circumstances forced later generations of rabbis to expand the corpus of Jewish texts. They responded to problems, some of which were particular to their time and place, through a process of interpretation, writing for other rabbis as well as for ordinary Jews who sought guidance on how best to conform to the laws of Judaism. Rabbis also edited prayer books, which structured public worship, and they redacted texts for home-based ritual, such as *haggadot*, for the observance of the springtime holiday of Passover.

Right: Initial-Word Panel of Psalm 114. *From the* Kaufmann Haggadah. *Late 14th century. Spain. Ms. A422 fol. 43r. Vellum. 8 3/4 x 7 1/2 in. Library of the Hungarian Academy of Sciences, Kaufmann Collection, Budapest.*

Opposite: Passover, *from* The Rothschild Miscellany, *fol. 155v, Northern Italy, c. 1450–1480. The Israel Museum, Jerusalem. This page depicts the search for leaven and the preparation of Matzah. Passover remains a favorite holiday among Jews. The Haggadah (literally, "the telling") narrates the liberation of the Israelites from their slavery in Egypt.*

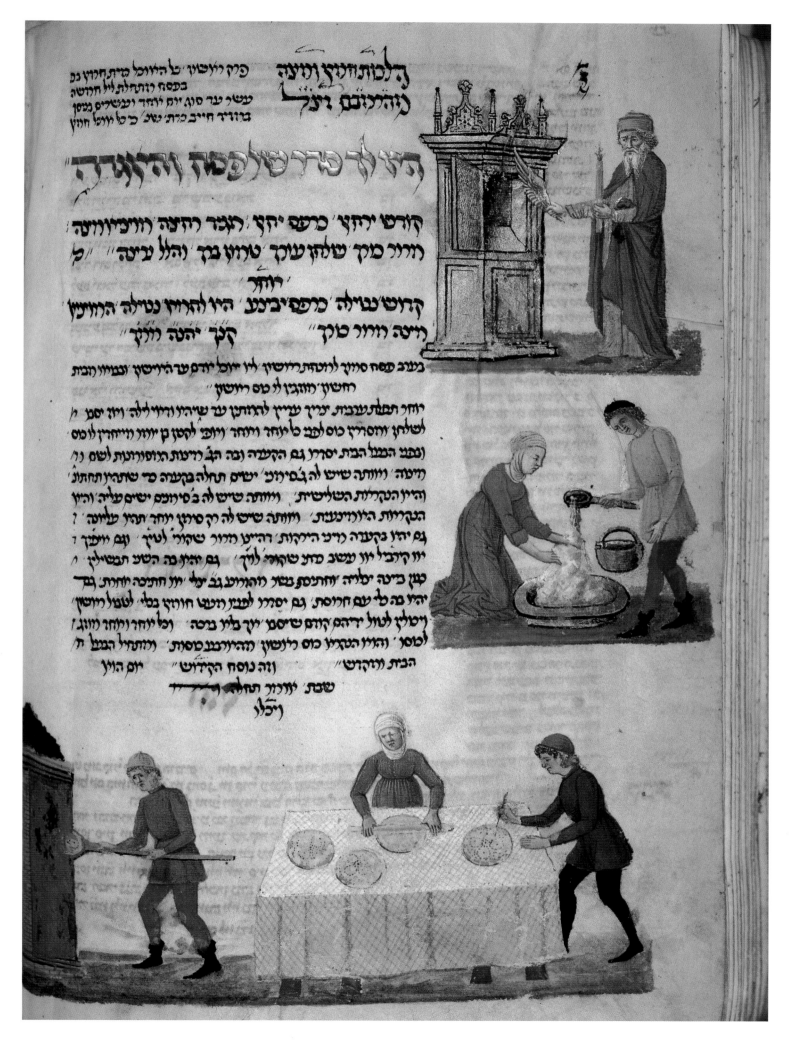

With their massive output of texts, rabbis vastly enlarged the body of literature used by "the people of the Book."

Over time new holy days were added to their calendars. The Bible fixed Passover, Succoth, and Shavuot as sacred days of pilgrimage and Rosh Hashanah and Yom Kippur as days of awe, when Jews were to submit themselves to self-evaluation and pray for repentance. Holidays such as Hanukkah and Purim, widely enjoyed as days of merriment and celebration, were added to the Jewish calendar centuries later. Their novelty did not make them any less central to the way Jews lived out the cycle of the year. The new holidays and those based on scripture, along with the regular weekly observance of the Sabbath, structured Jewish ideas about time.

Although Jewish history was always shaped by innovation and responses to new conditions, certain elements of that civilization remained relatively fixed. Jewish behavior took its basic shape from Jewish law, *halachah*. That law determined nearly everything about their daily lives, from their commitment to God, who had chosen them among all people, to how they related to the non-Jewish peoples around them.

Toward their fellow Jews they maintained, wherever they lived, an intense sense of obligation. As expressed in the Talmud, "All of Israel are responsible one for the other." In their communities, they used this principle to create elaborate communal structures to provide for the widowed, orphaned, sick, and distressed among them. Jewish communities maintained institutions to ensure proper burial, and to provide dowries for poor brides, inns for Jewish wayfarers, and interest-free loans for those in need of financial help; they set up poorhouses to feed the starving, and schools to usher boys into the Hebrew language and the details of religious knowledge.

They took seriously the ideas articulated in the Bible and the Talmud that defined them as a holy people, both separate and different from their neighbors. Much of their behavior—what they ate and how they dressed, adorned their bodies, buried their dead, married and established families, educated their children, and marked their calendars—intentionally distinguished them from their non-Jewish neighbors, whether they lived among pagans, Christians, or Moslems. In all historical settings, to be a Jew meant both something negative, not to be the adherent of another faith, and something affirmative, to count oneself as part of a transnational Jewish world.

Throughout most of their history Jews did not distinguish between themselves as adherents to a religious tradition and as a people bound to one another through the ties of community and nationhood. The idea of Israel as a people who had been chosen by God to receive and live by the Torah achieved integrity and coherence from the union of three elements: God, the divine; Torah, the law; and Israel, a holy community of people linked to one another across the generations.

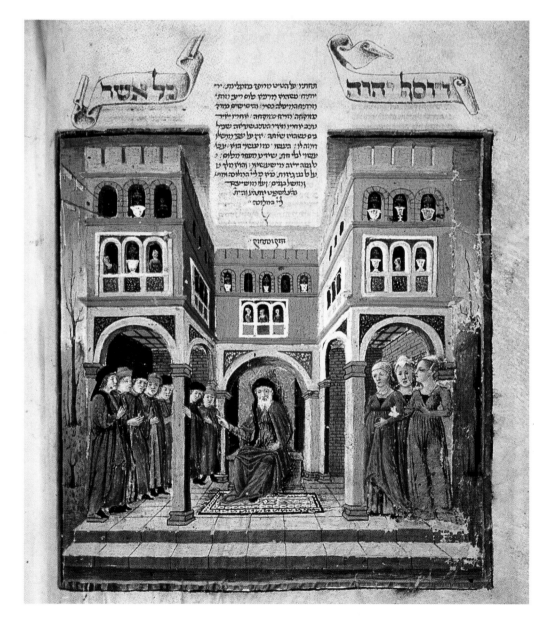

"And God Increased All" (from the Book of Job), The Rothschild Miscellany, fol. 64v. Northern Italy, c. 1450–1470. The Israel Museum, Jerusalem. The Rothschild Miscellany is the most extraordinary of illuminated Hebrew manuscripts. Commissioned in 1470, it is more than 900 pages and consists of 70 religious and secular texts.

They also did not mark sharp distinctions between home and community. Much religious life played itself out within the family. The rules governing the Jewish diet and the laws of family purity that regulated marital relations, for example, connected Jewish homes to Jewish communal institutions. Those practices operated along procedures articulated in the Bible and the Talmud and differed little from place to place and century to century.

However coherently Judaism tied together religion and peoplehood, the history of the Jewish people, including those who made their way to America starting in the middle of the seventeenth century, was shaped by constant wanderings across the face of the globe. Those migrations brought multiple variations into the commonality of the Jewish experience, as everyplace Jews lived, they adapted to the local environment.

In 586 B.C.E. they lost their homeland and were exiled to Babylonia. Although fifty years later they were allowed by new rulers to return and rebuild the Temple in Jerusalem, many remained in their place of exile in the land between the Tigris and Euphrates rivers. There they built a distinctive Babylonian Jewish civilization.

In 70 C.E. the Jews lost their national sovereignty once again and were subjected to exile at the hands of the Romans. From then on the Jews' history was one of constant migration and adaptation. While a skeletal Jewish population always remained in Jerusalem and a handful of other small communities in their holy land, most Jews submitted to exile.

At the outset, most of the world's exiled Jews lived around the Mediterranean basin, creating their own communities in Spain, Italy, North Africa, and Asia Minor. Over time, and primarily in pursuit of trade, they moved farther into Europe's heartland, establishing Jewish nodes in Germany, particularly up and down the Rhine River.

Wherever they settled they learned the languages of the people among whom they lived. They also picked up local styles of architecture to build their synagogues and other communal institutions. And they used local

Byzantine-period synagogue floor from Tiberias. The beautiful, intricate mosaic floors contained zodiacal and liturgical designs. The synagogue was destroyed during the fifth century C.E. The city of Tiberias was originally founded in 20 C.E. by Herod Antipas, and later became a major center of Jewish activity when the Sanhedrin, the council of Jewish law, moved there in the year 135 C.E.

ingredients to create Jewish food, usually producing dishes that resembled those of their neighbors while conforming to their own dietary restrictions.

Their ability to adapt to these new places stemmed in part from the fact that for many centuries Jews had been deeply involved in trade. While much of their commerce flowed along Jewish networks of exchange, they bought and sold goods to non-Jews, thus becoming intermediaries between classes and communities throughout much of the known world. Their commitment to their own tradition, however, with its emphasis on separateness and chosenness, made them notable wherever they resided. That is, they were willing to adapt in order to make a living, but they also wanted to be apart, to live as a community within a community.

Often this was no problem, and they frequently achieved a comfortable relationship with non-Jews. In some places they did so with great success. For a century and more in Spain, under the protection of Islamic rulers, Jews participated fully in the worlds of science, literature, philosophy, med-

Sounding the Shofar. Woodcut from a book of customs, Amsterdam, 1723. Sir Isaac and Lady Wolfson Museum, Jerusalem.

icine, law, and government while maintaining coherent Jewish communities that adhered closely to Jewish practice.

Yet at other times their aloofness was not tolerated. Particularly in the Christian world, with its emphasis on the singular truth of the Gospel and the problematic theological relationship between Judaism and Christianity, Jews experienced cycles of violence, mass killings, expulsions, and forced conversions. When economic and political disaster struck, Jews, so visibly different from the local majority, were handy scapegoats, blamed for plagues, wars, crop failures, or whatever other crisis loomed. In various places and times, they were required to wear distinguishing clothes or to live in ghettoes, were barred from owning land or belonging to guilds, and were subjected to inequitable taxation. Judaism as a religion was considered an inherently defective and evil faith.

The antipathy expressed by Christians toward Judaism and Jews went back to the earliest origins of Christianity. Jesus had been a Jew, as were most of his disciples. But Christian teachings blamed Jews for Jesus' death, and the refusal of Jews to accept the Gospel, the belief that they could achieve redemption by conversion, proved to be a terrible sticking point in their coexistence. Under Catholicism and then under Protestantism, brought into being when Martin Luther broke with the Church of Rome, Jews were excoriated for their unwillingness to see the truth and for their stubbornness in not accepting baptism.

Two dates ushered in major changes in terms of where Jews lived and how they understood themselves in relationship to the non-Jews who held political power, including the very power of life and death. In 1099 the fury of the Crusades uprooted many Jews from long-established French and German communities of the Rhine region. Those who survived the massacres perpetrated by the Christian soldiers bound for Jerusalem to liberate the holy city from the hands of the Moslems sought refuge in European lands farther to the east, creating early Jewish outposts in Poland, Lithuania, Bohemia, and Russia, a region that came to be known as Ashkenaz.

Rembrandt Harmensz. van Rijn. Jews in the Synagogue. *c. 1635. Etching on paper. 3 x 5 1/2 in. The Jewish Museum, New York. Gift of Dr. Harry G. Friedman.*

The year 1492 proved to be even more momentous in the history of the Jewish people. Under the edict of King Ferdinand and Queen Isabella, a millennium of Jewish life in Spain came to an end. The Jews of the Iberian peninsula, who had created one of the longest-lasting, most culturally dense, and institutionally richest Jewish communities anywhere, found themselves scattered over the globe, launching yet another diaspora.

Most of these Jews, known as Sephardim, or Spaniards, went to the Ottoman Empire; others showed up in Italy, Greece, and the south of France. Some made their way to cities in the German-speaking world that had expelled its Jews four hundred years earlier, and reestablished Jewish life on the fringes of the Atlantic.

A handful—those whose story represents the beginning point of the Jewish encounter with the Americas—made their way to what was then one of the most tolerant and religiously neutral places in Europe, the Netherlands.

In the early sixteenth century, the Netherlands was undergoing a vast expansion of its wealth and international reputation. The country was poor in natural resources, and its merchants understood that one way to com-

pensate for this deficit was to create an empire that could produce
revenues and add to its wealth. By
tapping into and controlling the
raw materials of the Americas,
Asia, and Africa, the Netherlands
became a superpower.

In 1621 the Dutch West India
Company had been chartered to
enable the Dutch to compete in
the lucrative trade of the New
World. By the middle of the cen-
tury, the small country on the
North Sea was poised to create
Europe's largest overseas empire.

The Netherlands' spectacular rise
in fortunes had powerful implications for the Jewish people, particularly for those who would in

1654 show up in the Dutch colony known as New Amsterdam, later to be
New York.

In 1492, during the reign of Ferdinand and Isabella, the Jews were expelled from Spain to promote the unity of Catholicism.

The Netherlands, a nation of devout Protestants, recognized the economic
benefit Jews would bring to its mercantile project. Jewish merchants,
refugees from Spain and Portugal, had trade connections with their
brethren all over the world. They could facilitate the Dutch quest for wealth
through their trade and connections in the far-flung Sephardic diaspora in
northern Europe, southern Europe, the Ottoman Empire, and the Levant.

The welcome the Jews received in Amsterdam had less to do with Dutch
commitment to religious tolerance or sympathy for Judaism—neither of
which the country had—than with a commitment to mercantile expansion. The authorities of the Netherlands allowed Jews into their communi-

ties, and in some places made it possible for them to practice their religion unimpeded, because they wagered that these Jews would be a boon to the nation's prestige and would add to its coffers.

Most Sephardic Jews who came to the Netherlands were *conversos*, Jews who had converted to Christianity in Spain and Portugal to escape persecution. Because the Dutch allowed them religious expression, at least compared to other Christian societies, many took advantage of this opportunity and learned anew what it meant to be Jewish. They built synagogues, consecrated Jewish cemeteries, hired rabbis, and printed Hebrew books. They also participated actively in the economic life of the Netherlands.

In 1624 a handful of Dutch Jews made a momentous decision. They joined Dutch Christians on a venture across the Atlantic to create a colony in Brazil, establishing themselves in the port of Bahia. In the next few years

Recife, Brazil, in the 1600s. The success of Jewish life in Brazil was facilitated by the policy of tolerance adopted by the Dutch West India Company. This liberal atmosphere in Recife was much like that enjoyed by Jews in Amsterdam.

Isaac Aboab da Fonseca, Rabbi of Amsterdam, 1686. Born in Portugal of a Marrano family, and educated in Amsterdam, Rabbi da Fonseca served in Brazil from 1642 to 1654.

Pernambuco and Recife, also Brazilian towns, were captured by the Dutch from the Portuguese, and among the women and men from the Netherlands who went there to make their fortunes were Jews.

As of 1645 about a thousand Jews had established themselves in Brazil. They constructed a synagogue, Zur Israel, to give public communal expression to their religious identity; and a rabbi, Isaac Aboab da Fonseca, came to Recife in 1642, the first rabbi in the Western Hemisphere.

This congregation, whose name translates as "rock of Israel," was the first established Jewish institution in the Americas, but life for the Jews of Brazil ended up built on a foundation less secure than a rock. When in 1654 the Portuguese reconquered Recife, the Jews, who had no desire to live under the rule of their former oppressors, fled. It was at this moment that the story of the Jews of what would become the United States began to unfold.

THE JEWISH SETTLEMENT
IN AMERICA
(1654–1776)

A lthough the twenty-three Jewish women and men who disembarked from the frigate *Sainte Catherine* into the rough and chaotic world of mid-seventeenth-century New Amsterdam were actually not the first Jews in the colony, they were the first group intending to establish a permanent Jewish settlement in America. These refugees from Brazil who ended up in New Amsterdam in September 1654 did not do so intentionally. They were fleeing the Portuguese in Brazil, and the *Sainte Catherine*, which was willing to take them, happened to be heading for the Dutch colony set at the mouth of the Hudson River, where it meets the Atlantic. They were greeted with considerable hostility by Peter Stuyvesant, governor of the colony and a devout member of the Dutch Reformed Church. He did not want the Jews to stay, claiming they would destroy the Christian character of the colony by practicing their "abominable religion," and their poverty would make them a burden to the community.

Stuyvesant conveyed these sentiments in a letter to his superiors in Amsterdam, the board of directors of the Dutch West India Company. The Jews in Amsterdam, on behalf of the new arrivals, also submitted a petition to the directors of the company. They pointed out that Jews had for decades been loyal to Dutch interests. They had been economically useful both at home and in the colonies, it was asserted, and in the worldwide competi-

Opposite: *Artist Unknown. Jacob Franks. c. 1740. Oil on canvas. 45 x 35 in. Gift of Captain N. Taylor Phillips to the American Jewish Historical Society, Waltham, Massachusetts, and New York, New York.* One of the wealthiest merchants in New York City, Franks served as parnas *(president) of* Congregation Shearith Israel *when its first synagogue was consecrated on April 8, 1730.*

Following spread: *Dutch merchant ships. 17th century.* By the mid-17th century, the Dutch empire in the western hemisphere stretched from today's New York to Brazil. Much of this territory was lost in wars during the second half of that century, particularly with England, over commercial interests.

The earliest view of New Amsterdam, 1651. Photo: © CORBIS. In 1654, the first Jews arrived in New Amsterdam, founded by Dutch colonists in 1625. After its conquest by England in 1664, the city was renamed New York. Its Jewish inhabitants were a mix of Sephardim and Ashkenazim, a notable feature of Jewish life in Holland as well. This particular demographic pattern would continue to distinguish American Jewry through the American Revolution.

tion raging between the Dutch and the Spanish, Portuguese, British, and French—all contestants for colonies and resources—the Jews and their trade connections had been, and could continue to be, very useful. The Jewish petitioners also pointed out that "many of the Jewish nation are principal shareholders of the company."

The argument of the Jews won out over those of Peter Stuyvesant. In April 1655 the directors in Amsterdam replied to Stuyvesant that "these people may travel and trade . . . and live and remain there." The victory for the Jews was not total, and the caveat included in the letter proved revealing. Yes, the Jews could remain, but they had to guarantee that they would be responsible for their own poor. Jews could never become public charges or burdens "to the company or to the community." In 1657 they were guaranteed the right of citizenship. They were allowed rights to engage in commerce and the right to own houses. Moreover, they could participate in the colony's very lucrative fur trade.

In 1655, Asser Levy, one of the original twenty-three refugees from Recife, Brazil, successfully petitioned the Dutch West India company for relief from

Stuyvesant's decision that Jews could not serve in the colonial guard, and, instead, must pay a special tax. Behind Levy's demand was a sense that Jews in this new colony should be able to serve the common good. Jews, Levy believed, would gain acceptance if they participated with their fellow residents of New Amsterdam in mutual support, rather than being stigmatized as different from other citizens.

Jews of New Amsterdam also asked for rights for their religious practices, such as the right to acquire land for cemeteries and to openly conduct worship services. In New Amsterdam, as in all the other European colonies in the New World, churches were established by civil authorities. In 1656, just two years after their arrival, the Dutch West India Company in Amsterdam once again sided with the Jews in opposition to Stuyvesant, telling them that they might "exercise in all quietness their religion within their houses." In that same year they formed themselves into a congregation, Shearith Israel (the name means "remnant of Israel"), which at the beginning of the twenty-first century still exists.

Not until decades later did Shearith Israel build a synagogue. As long as ten Jews were available to form a *minyan*, a quorum for prayer, worship could be held in a private house. According to Jewish belief, praying together makes a space sacred, not the façade of the building. In contrast, a Jewish cemetery has to be separate and consecrated, and it has to be outside the living area of a city or town. So within a decade of the establishment of the congregation of Shearith Israel, as more Jews moved to New Amsterdam (which became New York in 1664), they purchased land for a cemetery. That act was the first marking of Jewish space in North America.

These Jews also imported Torah scrolls for their religious worship, despite the lack of a synagogue building. They trained individuals within their growing ranks who could circumcise their sons eight days after birth, provide kosher meat by means of *shechita* (kosher slaughtering), educate their children, and lead services. Slowly, despite the hostility of Stuyvesant, the Jews of New Amsterdam/New York made themselves a home in America.

Jews in early America enjoyed greater liberties as individuals and as Jews than they did any place else in the Atlantic world, but those rights had not come to them automatically; rather, Jews had to argue for rights and prove that they would be useful to the colony. They had to offer a convincing reason for authorities to admit them, permit them to remain, and allow them to build their communities. Most of the argument hinged on trade and on the economic resources Jewish merchants would bring. A commercial people, the Jews had networks based on family and religion around the world. The assets they offered helped allay the negative reactions of Christians in New York and the other colonies where Jews would settle—Philadelphia, Newport, Savannah, and Charleston.

Notably, in this period before national independence, Jews chose to settle in those colonies offering the greatest religious freedom. Pennsylvania, founded by the Quaker William Penn, from the beginning was committed to freedom of expression for all believers in God. Roger Williams, founder of Rhode Island, had been banished from Massachusetts, a colony with an entrenched religious establishment. Williams, like Penn, conceived of a colony where religion was a matter of personal conscience. Jews settled in Philadelphia and Newport, commercial cities in colonies that did not link rights to beliefs and modes of worship.

By and large the American colonies were religiously much more diverse than the countries of Europe. The bitter, violent religious wars that had raged in Europe did not carry over to America. Thus, most Americans were relatively unbothered by denominational differences between themselves and their neighbors.

But conditions in Connecticut and Massachusetts were exceptions, and it is no wonder that few Jews settled there until well after the American Revolution. These bastions of Puritan conservatism were not hospitable to Jews, Catholics, and Quakers, who did not share the religious vision of the colonies' founders.

Even in colonies where they were generally welcome, Jews did not have full
civil equality, and were barred from
civic duties such as serving as jurors or
holding elective office. For example,
when members of the legislature
required an oath to be taken on a
Protestant Bible, neither Catholics nor
Jews could do it, because the swearing
would be meaningless. So though Jews
were somewhat circumscribed in their
civic participation, they were—unlike
in Europe—not the only ones.

The relative tolerance perhaps stemmed
from the newness of the colonial enterprise. In the young colonies, no one
group could claim significantly older

*Shearith Israel, the Spanish
and Portuguese synagogue in
New York City, founded in
1654. View of the open Ark
showing the Torah scrolls with
their multicolored cloaks, and
ancient bells made by Myer
Myers, well-known Jewish silversmith.*

roots than anyone else. Moreover, these colonies existed as sources of rev-
enue for England, and what tended to outweigh religious identity was one's
willingness and ability to produce goods and services that made a profit for
the colony. The colonies suffered from chronic labor shortages, and as a
result, most (white) people, regardless of religion, enjoyed a kind of equality by default.

Thus, it was within the context of an emerging society based on a nonide-
ological culture of religious tolerance, a place where privileges were allo-
cated along economic lines, that the earliest Jewish communities were
formed and flowered.

Notably, Jews living together in communities maintained a different exis-
tence than did Jews who ventured into American society as individuals or
families on their own, without benefit of a Jewish community. Jews showed
up in relatively remote outposts in the interior of the American colonies
early on; the occasional Jewish trader or shopkeeper could be found in the

backwoods of New York as far north as Albany, as well as in Pennsylvania, Virginia, and the Carolinas, selling goods to fur trappers, land speculators, and others in these isolated frontier settings.

Most Jews, however, lived in close communities in five cities: New York, Philadelphia, Newport, Savannah, and Charleston. In each Jewish community, a few wealthy merchants amassed fortunes in world trade, importing and exporting goods to and from ports around the globe. They linked the internal trade in furs and timber with the global trade in spices, and finished products from Europe. Trade counted for much in the colonies, and it is worth noting that each important Jewish community was situated in a thriving Atlantic seaport.

The vast majority of Jews were not wealthy, but most were involved in trade. They were shopkeepers and artisans—silversmiths, barrel makers, tin-

View of the junction of Pearl and Chatham Streets, New York, 1861. The site of the first Jews Burying Ground in New York City, maintained to the present day.

smiths—as well as sellers of food, candles, hardware, pots and pans, and other goods for daily use. Very few made a living from farming. Some were impoverished. Forty-two Jews came to Georgia in 1730, their fare paid by the Bevis Marks Synagogue in London. The poorer Jews in pre-Revolutionary America were typically not Sephardim, descendants of the Jews of Spain and Portugal. By the early eighteenth century Ashkenazim, Jews of northern and central European origin, and poorer than the Sephardim, had begun to come to America as well.

By 1720 a majority of American Jews were from Germany and Poland. Their history and migration to America differed from that of the Sephardim. They had not undergone the horrors of the Inquisition and expulsion, but neither did they have the same far-flung networks of trade that had enabled them to prosper.

These Jews came to America because the middle of the seventeenth century had been one of great hardship for the Jews of Poland. The Thirty Years' War (1618–1648), fought primarily between Catholics and Protestants, had savagely turned upon the Jews, who went through the most intense period of persecution since the Crusades. Tens of thousands were slaughtered, and even more lost their homes.

New York City as seen from Long Island. 18th century. In 1750 the Jewish population of New York City was estimated to be 300 persons. Ashkenazim (Jews of Western, Central, and Eastern Europe) became a majority of the New York Jewish community, even though Sephardic (Spanish and Portuguese) rituals were maintained.

A CLOSER LOOK:
AARON LOPEZ

When Aaron Lopez arrived in Newport, Rhode Island, in 1752 he did not carry that name—nor was he a Jew. His name in Portugal, where he came from, was Duarte Lopez, and publicly he practiced the Catholic faith. He was one of the *conversos*, Jews who had converted to Catholicism in order to remain on the Iberian peninsula during the Inquisition. But in the early eighteenth century, even Catholics of Jewish origin were no longer safe in Portugal, so Duarte and his brother Gabriel fled.

When Duarte and Gabriel arrived in Newport, they did two things. First they changed their names. Duarte became Aaron, and Gabriel took on the name Moses. They also submitted to circumcision as a way of publicly proclaiming their return to the Judaism of their ancestors. In 1767, another brother, Miguel, and his wife and children left Portugal, coming to America.

Aaron Lopez thrived in America, and became one of Newport's most prosperous merchants as well as an active and committed Jew. He built a veritable empire of commerce, maintaining a fleet of ships that sailed the world, bringing goods from North America to England, Holland, Sweden, Ireland, Spain, Portugal, the Azores, and the Canary Islands. His commercial sphere encompassed the Caribbean as well, and he dealt in sugar, oil, lumber, fish, flour, meat, textiles, spermaceti candles, and slaves. He built ships as well and sold them to others involved in the bustling trade that linked the ports of the Atlantic world.

Aaron Lopez, a survivor of the Inquisition, seemed to have viewed America as a place where he could prosper economically and where he was entitled to the same privileges as all other white men. In 1761, Aaron Lopez, along with Isaac Elizer, tried to take advantage of the 1740 Naturalization Act passed by Parliament, which allowed foreign-born men to become naturalized and therefore apply for citizenship. Lopez and Elizer applied in Rhode Island, where they lived, but the Rhode Island Assembly refused their petition on the grounds of their Jewishness. Then, the two took their petition to the next level, to the Rhode Island Superior Court, which once again rejected their plea, stating that the purpose of the colony was for "the free and quiet enjoyment of the Christian religion." Finally, Lopez slipped across the border to Massachusetts, where in 1762 he was granted his naturalization.

If the memories of the Inquisition seared themselves on Lopez's consciousness and made him assert his demand for the rights of citizenship, so, too, they structured his commitment to his Jewishness. He was an active member of Newport's Jewish community and its synagogue. When the British occupied Newport during the American Revolution, the Jews could not get kosher meat, which had up until then been imported. Lopez went for months without eating meat rather than violate Jewish practice.

Above: *Gilbert Stuart*. Sarah Rivera Lopez and Son Joshua. *c. 1775. Oil on canvas. 26 x 21 1/2 in. The Detroit Institute of Fine Arts.*

A sizable number of these Jewish refugees from Poland ended up in Amsterdam and London. The impoverished Ashkenazim who were in England and the Netherlands heard about the burgeoning economic opportunities for young people willing to work in the New World, and a number of them journeyed to America—some, like those who showed up in Georgia, sent through the largesse of these countries' Jewish communities, governed by the wealthy Sephardim.

In London and Amsterdam, Sephardim and Ashkenazim inhabited two separate worlds. While both groups acquired the dominant language, English or Dutch, among themselves, the Sephardim conversed in Portuguese, the Ashkenazim in Yiddish, the language of Ashkenaz, which was German written out in Hebrew characters. They had their own synagogues, cemeteries, and social lives. For centuries no intermarriages occurred between these two distinct classes of Jews. In America, on the other hand, these differences were gradually mitigated.

Charles Town, South Carolina, 18th century. The first Jew definitely known to have arrived in Charles Town was recorded as serving as interpreter of the governor. In 1749 the first congregation, Kahal Kadosh Beth Elohim, was organized. The Jewish population of Charles Town was about 200 in 1776.

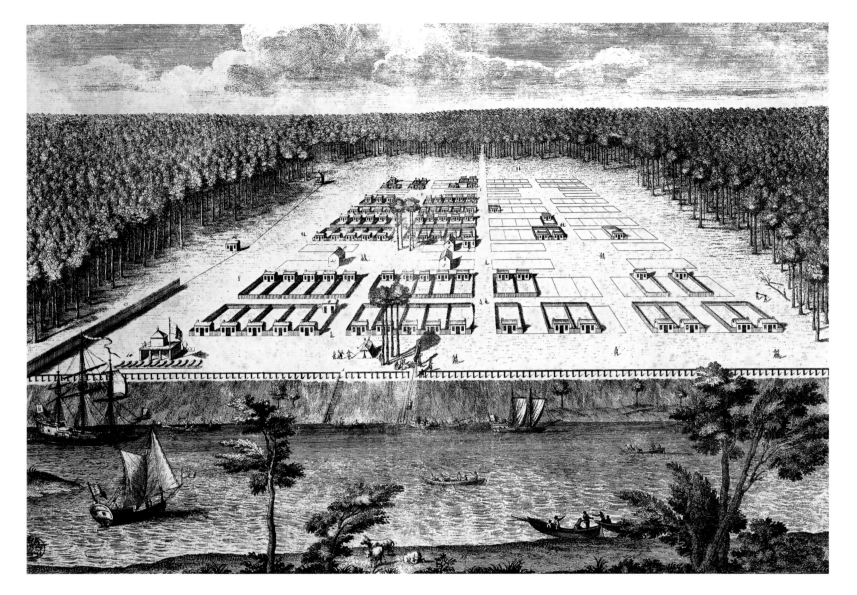

In each of the early American Jewish communities Sephardim and Ashkenazim shared a synagogue. They were buried next to each other in the city's sole Jewish cemetery. They married each other and gave charity to help each other. Their numbers were just too small and their communities too poor in institutions to be able to maintain such divisions.

The synagogue in early American Jewish communities—such as Mikveh Israel in Philadelphia or Mickveh Israel in Savannah—functioned as an all-purpose hub of Jewish life: a place for divine worship, Jewish education, and circumcision of sons. Here also, Jews were married, buried, and aided in times of distress. Kosher meat was distributed by the synagogue, as was *matzah* during Passover.

The fact that Jews needed the synagogue if they wanted to live as Jews gave a great deal of power to those who ran these institutions. It is notable that America did not yet have any rabbis. Rather, the synagogues were run by a

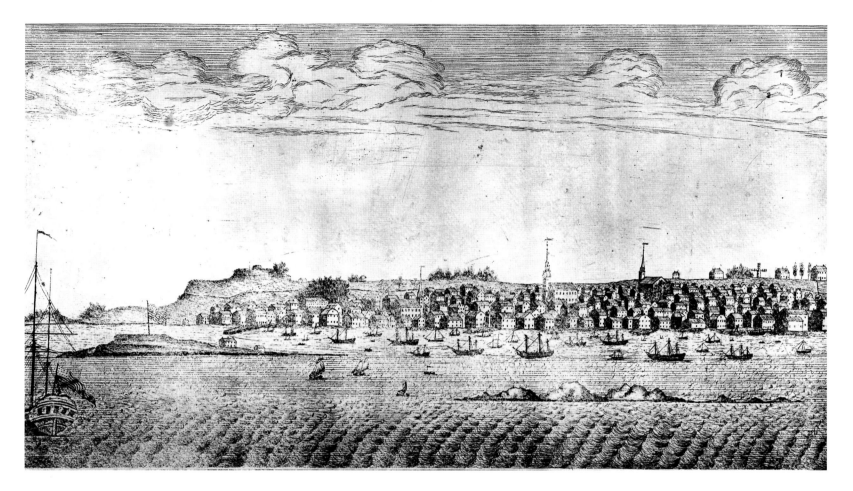

coterie of wealthy individuals, usually referred to as *parnassim*. The *parnassim* gave out honors and controlled access to the synagogue's services.

They attempted to enforce a kind of orthodoxy in practice, not just in the confines of the house of worship but in the Jews' private houses as well. If someone was accused of violating the Sabbath or eating unkosher meat, the *parnassim* would fine them. If the person refused to pay—as did a woman in New York, Hetty Hayes, who was suspected of serving *treife* (unkosher food) in her inn—the *parnassim* threatened to eject the individual from the community. Because each city had only one synagogue, and that synagogue functioned as the hub of the Jews' communal life, the threats were potent.

The absence of rabbis and the dire shortage of other Jewish functionaries had tremendous implications for the development of Jewish life in the American colonies. It was not a problem of conducting services, for Jews did not need rabbis to do that—any knowledgeable layman could chant the prayers, read from the Torah, officiate at funerals, and even perform marriage ceremonies. And most of the early American congregations actually employed one paid person, a *hazzan,* or cantor, to chant the service.

Southwest view of Newport, Rhode Island, 1795. In 1774, out of a total population of 9,000, the Jewish population of Newport was estimated at 200.

43

As rabbis had traditionally resolved matters of Jewish law, a variety of issues could not be adjudicated without them, at least according to standards of *halachah*. However, in early American Jewish communities, the *parnassim*—who had gotten their authority not by virtue of learning but because of their wealth—would often rule on such matters. They would be called in, for example, to decide if the child of a Jewish father and a non-Jewish mother could be buried in the Jewish cemetery. But the *parnassim* did not necessarily know the details of Jewish law, and their decisions were based on all sorts of extralegal considerations. Sometimes congregations wrote to rabbis in Amsterdam or London to decide for them, in effect making the American Jewish congregations colonial outposts of the larger Jewish communities.

The initial American Jewish communities were small—in 1700 about two hundred Jews lived in the British colonies of North America. Three quarters of a century later, on the eve of the American Revolution, their num-

The elegant Georgian-inspired exterior of Touro Synagogue in Newport, Rhode Island, designed by Peter Harrison, America's most famous eighteenth-century architect. Dedicated in 1763, Touro Synagogue is the oldest synagogue in America and the only one to survive from colonial days. Photo: © John Hopf Photography.

A CLOSER LOOK:
ABIGAIL FRANKS

Known to all as Abigail, Bilhah Abigail Levy Franks was born in London in 1688, the daughter of German-born Moses and Richea Levy. They moved to New York in 1695, and Abigail married Jacob Franks, a successful merchant, in 1712. They had nine children, born over the course of the twenty-seven years between 1715 and 1742. They belonged to Shearith Israel and played an active role in the life of the Jewish community of the city. Abigail Franks made sure that her children received instruction in the Jewish way of life. She observed the Sabbath and rigorously followed Jewish dietary laws. Yet she also socialized with non-Jews, whom she considered friends. She and her husband visited with them in their homes and maintained amicable relations across the previously impenetrable religious barrier. She read widely, consuming with pleasure the writings of Pope, Fielding, Addison, and Dryden. She was critical of what she saw as the superstitious elements within her own faith tradition and did not have much good to say about many members of New York Jewry, finding them to be frankly a "stupid set of people."

Abigail Franks has left us probably the most complete record of Jewish life in eighteenth-century America. She wrote voluminously to her son, who, like many colonial Jews, traveled on business around the Atlantic world. Her letters document the social, religious, political, and economic life of New York City and its Jews. In those letters we can see both the commitment of early American Jews to their religious tradition and their increasing comfort in a religiously mixed society. Her son Naphtali, for example, moved to England, she feared, for good. She was upset that he left and showed that in a letter written to him in 1741:

"I wish but for the happyness of Seeing you wich I begin to fear I never Shall for I dont wish you here And I amd Sure there is Little orbability of my Goeing to England. If parents would Give themselves Leave to Consider the many Difficulties that attendds the bringing up of children there would not be such Immoderate Joy att there birtth I dont mean the Care of there infancy thats the Least of its affter they arre gron Up and behave in Such a manner As to Give Sattisfaction then to be bereaved of them in the Decline of life when the injoying of them would be Our Greatest happyness for the Cares of giting a Liveing Ddisperses Them Up and

Bilhah Abigail Levy Franks. *c. 1740. American Jewish Historical Society, Waltham, Massachusetts, and New York, New York.*

down the world and the Only pleasure wee injoy (and thats internixt with Anxiety) is to hear they doe well Wich i A pleasure I hope to have."

An observant Jew in her home and in her congregation, Abigail Franks, like most of the elite of colonial American Jewry, was depicted in portraiture in the most modern clothing, without head-covering as mandated by Jewish law for married women and with the plunging neckline fashionable for women of the day. But when her daugher Phila married a gentile, Abigail refused to meet him, ever, and fell into a deep depression.

ber had grown tenfold, and about two thousand Jews greeted the Declaration of Independence.

Because their number was so small and among them were few individuals well versed in Jewish knowledge, they produced little in the way of a distinctive American Jewish culture. Most Jewish items they needed they imported. They did not print their own prayer books or *haggadot*. They had no rabbis whose words were added to the corpus of Jewish teachings.

Early American Jews made every effort to fit in. They dressed very much like other Americans of their class. The wealthiest among them had their portraits painted, and in those pictures they do not stand out from other comfortable eighteenth-century Americans.

The buildings they eventually constructed in America to house their congregations also fit into the local architectural landscape. Most of these first

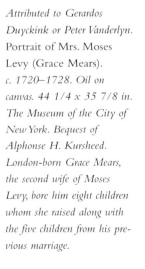

Attributed to Gerardos Duyckink or Peter Vanderlyn. Portrait of Mrs. Moses Levy (Grace Mears). c. 1720–1728. Oil on canvas. 44 1/4 x 35 7/8 in. The Museum of the City of New York. Bequest of Alphonse H. Kursheed. London-born Grace Mears, the second wife of Moses Levy, bore him eight children whom she raised along with the five children from his previous marriage.

synagogue buildings were constructed in the second half of the eighteenth century, and they followed the popular Palladian style, which was replete with pediments and columns, emphasizing the era's interest in elegance and symmetry. These buildings did not have any outward symbols of Jewishness on them: no Hebrew signs or words, Jewish stars, Ten Commandments, or any other Jewish symbol. For example, to the unaware who walked down the street in front of Jeshuat Israel, dedicated in 1763 in Newport, Rhode Island, the building would have seemed like most other public buildings in this bustling seaport. They could not know that inside, it was an exact copy, although smaller, of the great Spanish–Portuguese Synagogue in Amsterdam.

In summary, a blend of harmony with the outside world and conformity to the dictates of Jewish tradition characterized the early American Jews. They were not particularly secure in the enjoyment of the liberties that had been meted out to them in the colonies. They saw their good life in the American

Attributed to Gerardos Duyckink or Peter Vanderlyn. Portrait of Moses Levy. *c. 1720–1728. Oil on canvas. 42 1/2 x 33 1/2 in. The Museum of the City of New York. Bequest of Alphonse H. Kursheed. Levy was born in Germany in 1665, went to London and then to New York where he became a leader of the Jewish com-munity. The ship in the background symbolizes his immigrant beginnings and the international trade in which he was engaged.*

colonies as fragile and had no interest in calling attention to themselves as different from the Christian majority.

The age of the American Revolution and the emergence of the United States as a nation governed by a unique constitution grew out of this colonial legacy. The Jews who lived through the tumultuous decades of revolution and nation building did so mindful of their legacy of piecemeal acceptance and relative equality by default.

Headstone of Rebecca Polock, in the Old Jewish Burial Ground, Newport, Rhode Island. The most famous commentary on this site is Henry Longfellow's poem, "The Jewish Cemetery at Newport." Written in 1852, it both mourns and celebrates the fate of the Jews buried there.

Interior of Touro Synagogue, founded in Newport, Rhode Island, in 1658. The oldest existing synagogue in the United States, the building is a National Historic Site. Photo: © John Hopf Photography.

Lorado Taft. Memorial to Haym Salomon. *Chicago. 1936. Bronze. Height: 19 ft. 4 in. In times of crisis, American Jews liked to point to both their presence and their patriotism during America's founding moment. This monument was erected when anti-Semitism in the U.S. was high and European Jewry was suffering terrible persecution.*

THE DAWN OF A NEW REPUBLIC (1776–1820)

George Washington, newly elected president of the newly formed United States of America, paid a visit to Newport, Rhode Island, on August 17, 1790. While he was in Newport, officials of the local synagogue decided to greet him on behalf of the congregation. In their own name and that of all the Jews of America, they handed him a letter expressing their "cordial affection and esteem for your person and merits." They called upon Washington to remember that they, "the stock of Abraham," had for much of their history been "deprived . . . of the invaluable rights of free citizens." Therefore they had high hopes for "a Government erected by the majesty of the people."

While they made no specific requests of the president and the nation whose helm he was about to take over, the letter revealed their hope that the new government would protect them as it did all the rest of its citizens. It also implied that they were not certain as to what their status would be in the nation they had helped create.

Washington's reply to the leaders of the Newport congregation echoed their words and made a promise to the Jews of America. This new "good government" would offer, he wrote, "to bigotry no sanction, to persecution no assistance. "The children of the Stock of Abraham, who dwell in this land," will do well so long as they "demean themselves as good citizens."

American Jews have for over two centuries quoted this letter. They have focused on the phrase "to bigotry no sanction," to demonstrate that from the beginning Jews in America enjoyed a modicum of protection from the endemic hatred that had poisoned their lives in Europe. And, indeed, they have been justified in their telling of that history as one in which anti-Jewish sentiment resided only on the margins of society and the national government refrained from fostering the division of its citizens by religion.

From the time of the Revolution and early nation-building onward, American Jews lived with a sense that they had to prove themselves. They understood that their acceptance and prosperity hinged in part on the willingness of their non-Jewish neighbors to accept them. Would the majority Christian population find them too demanding, too concerned about their own needs, too clannish, too much part of the diasporic Jewish people and too little a part of the American people?

These kinds of worries plagued Jews from the end of the eighteenth century well into the second half of the twentieth century, and shaped how they participated in the Revolution and in the early development of the newly created United States. The smaller their numbers, the more such calculations informed their actions.

On the eve of the American Revolution, about two thousand Jews lived in the British colonies of North America. As mentioned earlier, most lived clustered in five cities: New York, Philadelphia, Newport, Charleston, and Savannah. Individual Jews lived elsewhere—in Virginia, Maryland, parts of New England, and the northern part of New York. These individuals might travel on occasion to the nearest city where a Jewish community existed, but by and large they functioned outside the orbit of organized Jewish life.

Generally, Jews in the Revolutionary era supported the cause of independence. Part of that support grew out of their economic profile. Jews were merchants. Some of them made a handsome profit from international trade, and others operated as small traders and craftsmen. But they were a commercial people whose livelihood depended upon the free flow of goods.

As such, colonists' complaints that the British were trying to overregulate American trade fell on sympathetic Jewish ears. The Proclamation of 1763, which banned Americans from engaging in trade beyond the crest of the Appalachian mountains, stifled commerce, and Jewish merchants had their eyes on the fur, timber, and other resources that lay beyond the line of demarcation.

Books & Stationary,

FOR SALE BY

BENJAMIN GOMEZ,

No. 97, MAIDEN-LANE.

Among which are the following:

The PRACTICAL NAVIGATOR, and SEAMAN's NEW DAILY ASSISTANT. Latest London Edition.

SEAMEN's JOURNALS.

Blank Books, Different Kinds.

ket Memorandum Books, Receipt Books, Copperplate Copy Books, best gilt quarto Writing Paper, common do. best foolscap do. common do. Wafers, Sealing Wax, Quills, Ink-Powder, Black Lead pencils, Ink-Stands, Slates, Playing-Cards, &c. &c. A great variety of NEW PLAYS and FARCES.

*** BOOK-BINDING carried on with neatnefs and difpatch.

The first American Jewish bookseller and publisher opened his shop in New York in 1791. Benjamin Gomez was the descendant of a Spanish Jewish family that arrived in this country at the beginning of the 18th century. Like other members of his family who were successful New York merchants, he was an active member of Congregation Shearith Israel, where he served as both its treasurer and president.

Few Jews in the colonies had come from England. Those who did were actually poor German and Polish Jews—*Betteljuden*, or Jewish beggars— who had briefly sojourned in England and were then shipped to Georgia so as to not be a burden on the *kehillah*, or "self-governing community." Therefore few, perhaps none, of the Jews harbored warm and positive feelings for the mother country.

When hostilities broke out, Francis Salvador of South Carolina, a Jew, was one of the first Americans to die for the cause. Solomon Bush, David Franks, and Benjamin Nones were also important figures. Enough Jews from South Carolina rallied to the cause of the patriots that they formed themselves into a special "Jew Company," and a Jewish doctor ministered to the medical needs of Washington's troops at Valley Forge. When the British put up a naval blockade of the port of Savannah, Mordecai Sheftell tried to break it. He was caught by the British, and after a brief incarceration on a prison ship, was exiled to their colony of Antigua.

Myer Myers. Cake Basket.
1760–1770. Silver.
Length: 14 1/2 in. The
Metropolitan Museum of Art.
Morris K. Jesup Fund,
1954. In colonial America,
most Jewish families resided
in urban centers, with the
men working as businessmen,
including craftsmen. Myers,
a New York silversmith, has
been ranked as the first signif-
icant Jewish artist in America.

The best-known Jewish hero of the Revolution was Haym Salomon, a Jew who had come to New York from Lissa, Poland, in the 1770s. Salomon did not have military prowess to offer the cause, but he helped in a different way. In the 1780s Salomon and a number of other Jewish "brokers" were attacked in the Pennsylvania legislatures in classical anti-Jewish language, as "despisers of Christianity." In the halls of the legislature and in the press, Salomon and the others were accused of putting their own financial interests above those of the public. Salomon rose, heroically, to the occasion. Rather than endure such attacks, he answered his critics: "I am a Jew; it is my own nation. . . . I exult and glory in reflecting that we have the honour to reside in a free country where, as a people, we have met the most generous countenance and protection."

In the years to come, when they felt under attack, Jews would cite their bravery and their support for independence. Benjamin Nones, for example, joined up with the Revolutionary cause immediately upon arrival in America from France in 1777. By the end of the century, he had become active in the politics of the Democrat-Republican Party in his adopted city of Philadelphia. When a newspaper advocating the cause of the rival

Federalists attacked him, he responded in a letter to the *Aurora*: "I am a Jew . . . as so were Abraham, and Isaac, and Moses and the prophets, and so too were Christ and his apostles. . . . I am a *Republican!* . . . I have *fought* as an American, throughout the whole of the revolutionary war. . . . I fought in almost every action which took place in Carolina."

For the Jews, however, the Revolution was not just about a handful of their heroes. The War for Independence left its mark on American Jewish life in a broader sense. When the British occupied New York, the *hazzan* of Shearith Israel, Gershon Mendes Seixas, along with the members of the congregation, fled. Taking their Torah scroll and the congregation's other ritual objects with them, the members of Shearith Israel relocated in Philadelphia with the help of the members of Mikveh Israel.

Haym Salomon has been celebrated by American Jews as a patriot and hero. Settling in New York in the 1770s, he remained in the city after it fell to the British, supposedly as an American spy. In the early 1780s, his work in financial markets secured important assistance for the Revolution.

While living in Philadelphia, Seixas, along with Haym Salomon and several other leaders of Mikveh Israel, petitioned the Pennsylvania Council of Censors, quietly protesting the fact that the state, newly created out of the former colony, required that anyone who would be elected had to take an oath. That oath required pledging allegiance and affirming belief in "the Scriptures of the Old and New Testament." No Jew could in good faith make that pledge.

The Jews' remonstrance pointed out to the state officials that if this wording was kept, many immigrants would shy away from Pennsylvania. Pennsylvania in particular had been an attractive destination for Lutherans, Quakers, Anabaptists, Pietists, Catholics, Presbyterians, and even women and men who had no religious affiliation. The linkage of religion and public ser-

Gershon Mendes Seixas, born in New York in 1746, was America's first native-born rabbi and for years the chief spokesman of American Jewry. The leader of Congregation Shearith Israel, he was also active with the Minutemen and in later years was elected trustee of Columbia College. Seixas was the first hazzan to have been born in America. He was the child of a Sephardic father and an Ashkenazi mother. Differences that would have made such a marriage unacceptable in Amsterdam and London were irrelevant in the face of American conditions.

vice would very likely send these diverse groups elsewhere. And, Seixas and Salomon pointed out, Jews had been fighting for independence and laying down their lives alongside their Christian neighbors. The Jews of Pennsylvania, they claimed, had earned the right to hold office as well as the right to be full and equal citizens, since some of them had fought in the Continental Army and "some went out in the militia to fight the common enemy; all of them have cheerfully contributed to the support of the militia and of the government of this state."

This plea for consideration echoed throughout early American history. Jews wanted equal rights—the right to have their religious traditions protected, the right as citizens to hold government office and participate in politics—and they asked for it, in large measure by invoking their service to the Revolutionary cause and, later, their service in other wars.

These pleas took on particular urgency in the immediate aftermath of the Declaration of Independence. The states, now freed from British rule, began to think about the nature of citizenship and write constitutions. New York in 1777, for example, guaranteed complete religious freedom to anyone who lived there. Virginia, which already had a small Jewish population in Richmond, disestablished religion in its first state constitution of 1775. Other states took longer. Maryland limited office holding to Christians until the early 1820s, when that state's legislature passed the "Jew Bill." Massachusetts also connected serving the public with professing Christianity until the 1820s. Georgia, New Hampshire, and North Carolina actually required a statement of belief in Protestant Christianity.

These restrictions were actually not aimed at Jews. States were more concerned about "nonbelievers" than they were about Jews, and in those places that limited the holding of office to Protestants, Catholics were considered a significantly greater threat than Jews.

That different states had different policies regarding religion and its relationship to public life grew out of the nature of the U.S. Constitution, a document that has profoundly impacted the history of the American

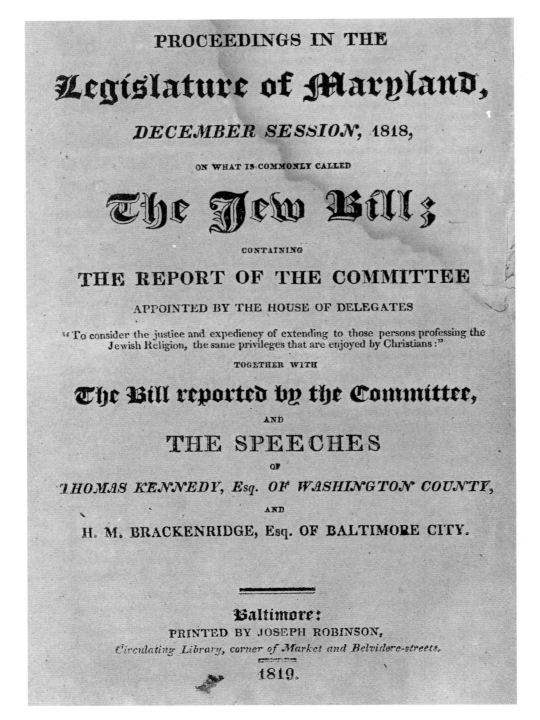

Report of the debate on the Jew Bill, published in 1819, to Jews in Maryland. Seven years later the bill was finally passed. In this regard, Maryland was not exceptional. Old colonial charters and even constitutions passed by states during the Revolution often excluded Jews from civic equality. In some, franchise and office-holding were restricted to Protestants or Christians. Others required an oath to Christian principles.

PROCEEDINGS IN THE

Legislature of Maryland,

DECEMBER SESSION, 1818,

ON WHAT IS COMMONLY CALLED

The Jew Bill;

CONTAINING

THE REPORT OF THE COMMITTEE

APPOINTED BY THE HOUSE OF DELEGATES

"To consider the justice and expediency of extending to those persons professing the Jewish Religion, the same privileges that are enjoyed by Christians:"

TOGETHER WITH

The Bill reported by the Committee,

AND

THE SPEECHES

OF

THOMAS KENNEDY, Esq. OF *WASHINGTON COUNTY*,

AND

H. M. BRACKENRIDGE, Esq. OF BALTIMORE CITY.

Baltimore:

PRINTED BY JOSEPH ROBINSON,

Circulating Library, corner of Market and Belvidere-streets.

1819.

Jewish people. The Constitution enumerated, particularly in Article II, what Congress could and could not do. It left great latitude to the individual states. For state and local elections, the states had the right to determine qualification of candidates. The U.S. Constitution specified qualifications only for those holding national office—serving in the House of Representatives, the Senate, and the presidency. Article VI, section 3, declared that "no religious test shall ever be required as a qualification to any office or public trust under the United States." However, the states were free until 1865 to set their own standards, and a few states—Maryland, New Hampshire, and North Carolina—maintained restrictions on Jewish participation.

The most important part of the Constitution in terms of Jewish rights and the evolution of the history of the Jews in America was contained in the Bill of Rights, particularly the First Amendment, which was adopted immediately upon ratification of the Constitution. That amendment had two clauses that shaped the history of the Jews of America: "Congress shall make no law respecting an establishment of religion, or prohibiting the free exercise thereof." The free-exercise clause gave Jews a legal basis to protest when they believed that federal policy made it impossible for them to practice their religion freely. The nonestablishment clause made it unconstitutional for the federal government to support one religion over another.

While jurists and constitutional scholars have argued for centuries over exactly what these words mean and how they should be put into practice, at the time, they provided a powerful guarantee for Jews that their religion would not make them less worthy than other Americans.

Still, during several episodes in the history of America's Jews, the government's behavior seemed to contradict the words of the Constitution and those of George Washington in his 1790 letter to the congregation in Newport. In 1813, for example, Secretary of State James Monroe wanted to have Mordecai Manuel Noah, probably the most prominent American Jew of the early nineteenth century, removed from his diplomatic posting in Tunis. Monroe wrote to Noah asserting that "the religion which you profess" was hampering "consular functions." Noah and a number of other American Jews protested in print. Religion, they wrote, should make no difference in public life, only "one great character of *citizenship* . . . prevails."

Despite these episodes, American Jews enjoyed greater political rights than any other community of their brethren anyplace in the world. Unlike Jews in England and France, they never had to be emancipated. The words of the U.S. Constitution made it clear—despite subsequent sporadic lapses—that religion was a matter of private concern, not the government's.

For Jews, the two constitutional clauses on religion created an environment that was compatible with innovations in religious practice. Since the gov-

In the midst of his busy career in New York politics and journalism, Mordecai Manuel Noah made the time to work on behalf of the Jewish people. He was one of the earliest American Jews to call for the creation of a college to train American Jews in the classic texts of their tradition, and worked to create a Jewish agricultural settlement to help some of the Jewish poor in New York. His grandest—and most unattainable—scheme was Ararat. In 1820 he purchased Grand Island, an island near Niagara Falls. He envisioned it as a refuge for Europe's oppressed Jews. He was to be its leader, and here Jews could escape the violence and poverty of the Old World.

ernment was not interested in the inner workings of any religious community, and the clergy received no support or power from the state, the members of such communities, rather than the clergy, had the power to shape religious practice. Thus, in the era of the Revolution and the writing of the Constitution, Jewish communal institutions in America underwent their own internal revolution.

Members of congregations demanded that their religious bodies also be governed by constitutions and that they adopt more egalitarian procedures. They stripped the *parnassim* of much of their power and put the affairs of the congregations into the hands of officers democratically elected by all adult males. Further, some congregations moved away from seating assigned on the basis of economic status. Moreover, as new synagogues were established, they broke the monopoly each city's sole synagogue had enjoyed since the end of the seventeenth century. In 1802 some Philadelphia Jews broke away from Mikveh Israel to found Rodeph Shalom, the first congregation in America to follow *minhag Ashkenaz*, the German rite. In New York, B'nai Jeshurun was founded by central Europeans, breaking the stranglehold the Sephardim had on American Judaism.

These additional congregations represented the growing will of the majority to shape their own institutions. By the eve of the Revolution, more American Jews were Ashkenazim than Sephardim. As Americans, the Ashkenazim believed that institutions should function by the "consent of the governed." They did not give their consent to a style of prayer and an institutional language—Portuguese—that did not represent who they were.

A third factor that changed Jewish institutions in the early United States was the physical growth of American cities in the period following the Revolution. For example, as New York and Philadelphia expanded in population and physical size, many Jews, like their neighbors, moved to new neighborhoods. In these new parts of the city, Jews established homes, businesses—and new synagogues. These new synagogues began to compete with the older ones for members.

Also late in the eighteenth century, Jews in New York, Charleston, and Philadelphia began to create Jewish institutions outside the synagogue. The first was probably Charleston's Hebrew Benevolent Institution, founded in 1791. Until then charity in its various forms had emanated from the synagogue and was available to members, an entitlement of belonging. But the development of charitable societies, then schools, and eventually social institutions outside of synagogues meant that Jews in America could function as Jews without belonging to synagogues. This threatened the centrality of the synagogue to Jewish life. It also opened up the possibility that some Jews, perhaps large numbers, would derive their sense of community and fulfill many of their needs of Jewish life without joining a synagogue, paying dues, and participating in worship. This shifted the power from the synagogue to the laity, who, if they did not like the synagogue or (eventually) its rabbi, could quit, leave for another synagogue, or simply utilize other Jewish institutions.

By the start of the 1820s, Jewish life in the port cities hugging the Atlantic was being significantly transformed. The influx of immigrants from central Europe shook up the small, inconspicuous urban Jewish communities, greatly expanding their population and transforming the nature of American Jewish culture.

Beginning in the 1810s individual Jews had also begun to make their way west, journeying over the Appalachians in search of trade. These first few individuals were soon joined by others, and in 1819 the first congregation outside the eastern seaboard was founded in Cincinnati.

For the next century, the story of the Jewish people in America was shaped by the continuous arrival of immigrants from Europe. These newcomers shook up the old communities, built new ones, and tested the delicate balancing act that had been a way of life for the Jews of the Revolutionary and nation-building era.

The design of the Seal of the Hebrew Benevolent Society of Charleston shows the figure of a skeleton representing the Angel of Death with a scythe in the right hand and an hour glass in the left. The original name of the society is engraved in Hebrew, "Hebra Gemilut Hasadim" ("Society for Deeds of Loving Kindness"). The biblical motto of the society also appears. Under the figure of the Angel of Death is the Hebrew "Tsadakah Tatzil Mi-Mavet" ("Charity Delivers from Death": Proverbs 10:2).

Congregation Beth Elohim, Charleston, South Carolina. The exterior of this 1795 synagogue was destroyed by fire in 1838. When the synagogue was built, Charleston was the largest Jewish community in the United States. The first initiative by American Jews for religious reform came in Charleston, in 1825, when the "Reform Society of Israelites" broke away from this congregation.

BECOMING AMERICAN JEWS (1820–1880)

About two thousand Jews lived in America in 1820. As they had during previous decades in this country, they shied away from attention, and they asked relatively little from American society. But sixty momentous years later, when their numbers stood at about a quarter of a million, they boldly proclaimed their presence in their communities, and they made clear in their behavior that they had specific needs as Jews.

That their number increased over a hundredfold had little to do with high levels of fertility. Although these women and men did in fact have large families, the skyrocketing Jewish population in the United States resulted from the "America fever" that swept through the Jewish communities of central Europe.

From Alsace in the west into western Russia and Lithuania in the east, the idea spread that America represented a reasonable alternative for Jews. Through newspapers, books, reports of travelers, and letters from family members, the word *America* came to stand for a place where Jews could live freely and prosper.

At the beginning of these six decades, going to America was a courageous act, a decision taken primarily by the young and the adventurous. While

Opposite: Betty Kohn Wollman, Jewish pioneer in Kansas, was visited at her home in Leavenworth by Abraham Lincoln in 1859. In 1862, General Ulysses Grant, impatient with smuggling, issued an order to expel Jews from the territory under his command. Lincoln, when made aware of the order, revoked it.

most Jews did not make the move to America, many did, and their decision left its mark on both American society and on those Jews who stayed put. Over the course of these years, the migration to America transformed central European Jewry, which sent large numbers of its young and its poor across the Atlantic.

By the 1880s, the idea of transplanting oneself to New York, Cincinnati, San Francisco, Chicago, or virtually anyplace in the United States had become a fairly common option for European Jews. By that decade, young Jews who abandoned their hometowns in Germany, Hungary, Austria, Bohemia, Moravia, Poland, and Lithuania no longer were being lured by the spirit of adventure. Indeed, most came to America with family members and townspeople already there, able to teach them the intricacies of American culture.

Polish immigrants being processed before traveling to the United States.

*Judah Touro of New Orleans,
one of America's most
renowned philanthropists,
around 1854. An Orthodox
Jew, he refused to remove his
hat for the portrait. Touro is
remembered today for the
Touro Synagogue in
Newport, Rhode Island, once
the home of Congregation
Yeshuath Israel. He grew up
in Newport, and, despite
moving to New Orleans,
generously bequeathed funds
to the synagogue in his will.*

By 1880 Jewish communities large and small existed in almost every state
of the Union. A few Jews had become fabulously wealthy. This handful,
who called themselves "our crowd," lived opulently and enjoyed great prestige and influence in American society. Most Jews, however, made a solid
living in small business, particularly dry-goods. Compared to Jews in much
of Europe, they lived in harmony with their American neighbors and
enjoyed complete political equality, without the specter of anti-Semitism
looming large in their daily lives.

How did this transition take place? How did the small American Jewish
community that existed on the Atlantic seaboard in 1820 become so large,
influential, and well developed?

The answers to these questions can be found on both sides of the ocean, in
those forces that propelled outward almost two hundred thousand Jews and
the forces in America that drew them in.

For the first part of the equation, Europe, we can turn to the worsening economic position of many Jews. Europe was going through an industrial revolution, a dramatic modernization of its economy. The railroad was bringing finished goods into the hinterlands of central Europe, and it was taking agricultural goods to the cities, where they would be consumed.

Watercolor of Dr. Albert Moses Levy at the Siege of Bexar, San Antonio, Texas, 1835. Bruce Marshall, artist. Levy (1800–1848) was appointed surgeon-in-chief for the Texas volunteer army in 1835. In 1986, a memorial day in his name was instituted in Houston to honor Jews who fought for Texas independence.

The transformation of the European economy had a significant impact upon the Jews. For centuries Jews had been traders, brokering between the peasants who grew crops and the merchants who brought them to market. Jews not only bought wheat, flax, timber, grapes, and other items that needed to be transformed for usage; they sold finished products—flour, linen, wood, wine—to agricultural laborers. Most of them did this at the lowest rung of the commercial economy, as peddlers. Some had enough resources to own a horse and wagon and handle larger stocks of goods.

But no matter the level at which they operated, they were threatened by the coming industrial economy. The railroad could bring those same goods to the hinterlands more efficiently and more cheaply than the Jewish traders could. Railroads and improvements in transoceanic travel made it cheaper to ship wheat from the American Middle West to Europe than to bring it from the agricultural regions of central Europe to the big cities. In this way, the encroaching industrial revolution in large part wiped out the Jews' economic niche in Europe

Some Jews in Europe benefited from this era of technological progress. Those who had some capital and knew the language of the country could leave the small towns where most found themselves at the beginning of this era and move to the cities—Berlin, Vienna, Paris, Strasburg, Prague, Budapest, Frankfurt, Warsaw, Breslau—where the real development was taking place. Here, with some money, they could open mills, factories, warehouses, and workshops to produce goods, or stores to sell to the growing urban population. A few opened grand department stores, patronized by the middle classes.

Watercolor of Morris Lasker making a sale. San Antonio, Texas. Bruce Marshall, artist. Before 1821, when Texas was a Spanish colony, legal residence was limited to Catholics. By 1860, there were Jewish communities in Galveston, Houston, and San Antonio.

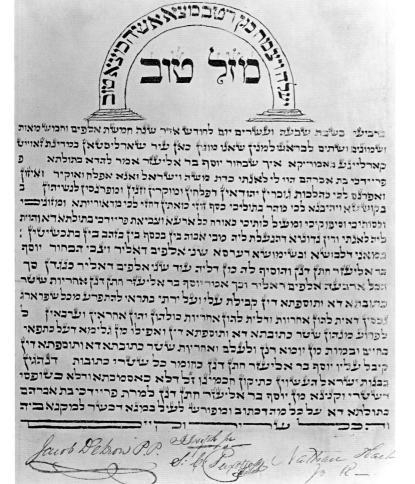

Hebrew marriage certificate, Charleston, South Carolina, 1822. The traditional Jewish certificate of marriage, the ketubbah, *is one of Judaism's oldest legal documents.*

Some less-well-off Jews went to the cities to work as clerks and artisans. Young Jewish girls went to the cities to work as servants in the homes of wealthier Jewish families. Both groups hoped that the educational opportunities in the cities would lead to better lives for their children.

This urban movement and the hopes that so many Jews pinned on education took place as central European Jews went through the process of emancipation. A long and drawn-out affair, emancipation meant that the states decided that Jews, or at least some of them, should have the rights of citizenship. No longer were all to be treated as members of an inferior class or group. Rather, the state began to allow some Jews the same rights as other individuals.

In much of central Europe, emancipation was tied to education. In Germany, for example, Jews were awarded rights of citizenship if they could prove that they knew German, had some financial means, and in general conformed to German expectations of behavior. But among central Europe's Jews, many were too poor and too unconversant with the language of the larger society to successfully make the move to the bigger cities and participate in the quest for emancipation.

In many central European states, the lives of Jews were not only limited economically. Other kinds of restrictions impoverished their lives as well. Bavaria, for example, from which so many Jews came to America, restricted the number of Jews who could marry. No one was allowed to marry unless a legal, official place existed for them in the community, and for the poor, such places became available only when someone died. Thus, to remain in Europe meant basically to go without work and to be unable to marry, have a family, and live as an adult.

The details of Jewish emigration from central Europe to America—who left, where they went, and how they made the trip—reveal much about the emigrants and their expectations and experiences in America.

In the early years the emigrants tended to be young. Although some, decades later, brought an elderly mother or father to America, the emigration of young adults to America meant that families were torn asunder. Letters went back and forth across the ocean. Children who did well in America frequently sent money to their kin in Europe, but in most cases they never saw each other again.

The young people who left tended initially to be men. Typically, a young man made the decision that he had no future in Europe. He went to America, primarily through the great ports in Hamburg, Bremen, Antwerp, or Rotterdam, at first by sailing ship. By the 1880s the journey to America was by steam. It took less than two weeks, and although the voyage was rough, people traveled in family units. They brought their own food so that they could observe the laws of *kashrut*. Certainly there were traumas. Families ran out of food and they had to eat what was provided on the ship. Young women complained of harassment. But the brevity of the journey and the lure of America spurred them on.

With the address of a relative or fellow townsperson in his pocket, a young immigrant on board ship might meet another Jewish young man, from a village not unlike his own. Together they would plan how to establish themselves in America. If they lacked personal contacts in America, they tended to seek out the local Jewish community in their port of entry— New York, Philadelphia, New Orleans, Boston, or Baltimore. After the discovery of gold in California in 1849, a steady stream of young Jewish men from Poland headed for the Pacific coast. Most went on ships bound for Panama, then took the overland route across the narrow isthmus, which brought them to ships heading for San Francisco.

In all the U.S. cities, they made contact with the Jews who already lived there. Here they heard familiar languages and interacted with people who observed the same holidays, who ate the same kinds of foods, and whose way of life was familiar.

Showing up in any one of the Jewish communities also helped them start earning money and establishing themselves in America. The Jews who were already established were deeply involved in trade, in the buying and selling of clothing, stoves, glass, needles, threads, buttons, bows, pens, pencils, dishes, and pots and pans. Thus, Jewish wholesalers outfitted these new immigrants with merchandise that they gave them free of interest, following a long-standing Jewish tradition of *gemilas hesed*, literally, "acts of loving kindness." The new immigrants learned from other Jewish peddlers how to say a few phrases in English, phrases relevant to the merchandise they carried. And then they were on their way, selling in the cities as urban peddlers, in the outskirts of the city, or in the vast hinterlands of rural America.

Jewish immigrants in this period clustered in different parts of the peddling field. For example, Russian Jewish immigrants in New York in the 1850s

Advertisement for Feustmann & Kaufmann, about 1860. In addition to being involved in retail trade, Jewish merchants were active in wholesale dry goods in cities along the eastern seaboard, the Midwest, and the California coast. Firms such as this one in Philadelphia often supplied peddlers that traveled by foot with packs or with horses and wagons to rural areas.

tended to go into the glass business. Up and down the streets of Manhattan, they intoned the only English words they knew: "Glass put in."

Those who peddled in the city had a good deal of competition, but they also had a dense network of community life. They lived close to other Jewish immigrants, usually building their social life around the neighborhood, the synagogues (which were multiplying in number), the taverns and cafés, and the Jewish lodges and benevolent associations.

In New York in 1843 twelve young Jewish men, all relatively recent immigrants, founded an organization that would last into the twenty-first century, B'nai B'rith, or "sons of the covenant." These young men had been rejected by the Masons for membership in their lodge and decided to found a similar organization for Jewish men. The organization provided not just fellowship for Jewish men, but also mutual assistance, burial insurance, and survivors' benefits for widows and orphans. In addition, B'nai B'rith became very active in providing relief to Jews in distress. It founded orphanages and old-age homes, and sent funds to help Jews who had lost their homes in the great Chicago fire of 1871.

C. G. Bush. The Peddler's Wagon. c. 1850. The peddler's hooked nose indicates that a Jew is showing clothing to these farm folk. Jewish peddlers were a common sight in rural as well as urban areas. Many borrowed money from friends, family, or other Jews to begin operations. Later, having accumulated some capital, they might open stores.

Downieville, 1856, one of the many mining towns in the hills of California where Jewish businessmen provided necessary services.

Those immigrants who made their way to the countryside went everywhere: the Midwest, New England, the Mississippi Delta, the Ohio River Valley, the Far West, the Southwest. They showed up, packs on their backs, to serve the farm families. Unlike their urban counterparts, these Jewish peddlers on the rural roads had little competition. But they also had little in the way of community.

They tended to peddle on their own during the week, sleeping in fields or, if they were lucky, in a barn. On Fridays they tried to get back to the nearest Jewish community. Even small towns housed a handful of Jewish families, and it was considered an obligation and honor for those families to host peddlers for the Sabbath. The peddler would sit down with the family for a Sabbath meal, rest on the seventh day, and on Sunday morning go back on the road.

The important turning point in the lives of these peddlers was when they had saved enough money to not only pay back the wholesalers who had given them goods to sell, but send money to their families in Europe to pay for their migration. Over the course of a decade or so, reasonably successful peddlers brought their brothers over and re-created an important part of their family in America. Having other family members present must have mitigated the isolation and loneliness that so many of them felt.

Working with one or more family members also meant being able to cover a bigger territory, thereby reaching more customers and selling more goods. This then made it possible to move up to owning a horse and wagon. The most successful peddlers squirreled away enough of their earnings to open small stores in small towns.

Throughout much of rural America in the nineteenth century, Jewish stores, usually offering sundries and dry goods, were a fixture of community life. In larger cities as well, successful peddlers opened stores, ending their days on the road. Often these new store owners in turn sponsored new immigrants, who took to the road to serve the rural population that could not easily get to town.

The act of putting down one's pack and becoming a shopkeeper heralded another crucial moment in the lives of these Jews and in the Jewish communities they would construct. Once a man abandoned the life of a peddler, he could marry.

Sometimes young men who went back for a visit to their European town of origin, to see parents and show off how America had changed them, could also find a young Jewish wife among the women of the town. Those who brought back a European Jewish wife often also brought back to America the sisters and cousins of their brides. These women married other Jewish bachelors, who made up a substantial portion of the Jewish population in America.

That so many Jews—the vast majority—made a living as shopkeepers influenced their relationships with the non-Jews among whom they lived, for merchants depended on the good will of their customers. Thus, Jews became active in the civic life of their towns. Many Jews in the West, Midwest, and South served as town officials, and the stability and order of the local community helped them to make a living. It was important for them to demonstrate that they did fit in socially, and even though they held fast to their own religious traditions, they did not want to differ radically from the majority.

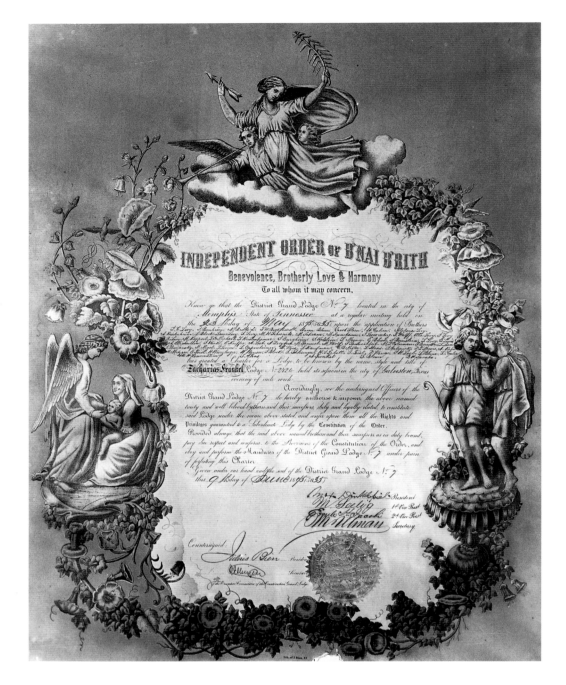

Charter of the benevolent society, The Independent Order of B'nai B'rith, Galveston, Texas, June 9, 1875. The first B'nai B'rith was founded by German Jews in New York, in 1843. Originally called the Bundes Brueder, its name was changed several years later to a Hebrew equivalent when a second such society appeared in Cincinnati.

The settling down of so many immigrant Jews in the nineteenth century also resulted in the growth of Jewish community life in America. Previously, many peddlers had lived as Jews, but because of their itinerant lifestyle, did not participate extensively in community life.

Once they married and had children, however, they began to focus on their need for synagogues, religious education, and burial services. They found ways to help the poor among themselves, to provide assistance to widows and orphans, and to help newcomers in need of work. And perhaps most important, these communities provided the basis for social life for the Jews and a setting in which to enjoy holidays and life cycle events.

In most towns, even relatively small ones, Jews formed congregations. Initially they worshiped in someone's home, the back of a shop, a rented hall, or even in a tavern. At some point in the history of most communities other than the very smallest, members decided that the congregation needed a building of their own. It seemed wrong for other denominations to worship in fine buildings while Jews gathered in the back of dry-goods stores to usher in their holy days. The first buildings were sometimes churches that were no longer in use, and this decision to reuse churches had an impact on the form of Judaism in America.

Churches and synagogues were designed differently. In synagogues a reader's stand occupied a central space among the male worshipers. It was from here that the Torah was read. Churches had only the pulpit in the front of the congregation. Also, churches usually had organs built in, whereas Jews had stopped having instrumental music in their services when the great Temple in Jerusalem was destroyed in 70 C.E.

Even more significant was the fact that churches did not have discrete sections set aside for women and men. Jews for centuries had conducted their religious services with women and men separated, men in the front and women either in the back or in a balcony.

When congregations purchased old churches, they had to decide what to do about these architectural and religious problems. Increasingly, most opted for doing away with separate seating. In America in the nineteenth century, much of Jewish religious life pivoted around women, and so separate seating no longer seemed to make sense.

As Jews in America made these decisions about how to orchestrate religious services, similar intellectual debates were raging in Germany. And as more Jews in Germany were being exposed to secular education, particularly at the university level, a great internal Jewish crisis was forming. More and more young Jewish men bound for the rabbinate were exposed to ideas that challenged traditional Judaism. Many German Jews were also

A CLOSER LOOK:
JEWS IN SAN FRANCISCO

The first large contingent of Jews showed up in San Francisco after the discovery of gold in 1849. To the gold fields, and the budding town of San Francisco, came Jewish peddlers who sold food, dry goods, and other equipment to the miners searching for gold. On Yom Kippur 1849 the rough-and-tumble town had enough Jews to hold two different religious services. Some Jews attended a predominantly Polish service, while others gravitated to one made up primarily of Germans. The former formed themselves into Congregation Shearith Israel in 1850, while others founded Congregation Emanu-El that same year, both of which still exist.

Certainly the most famous Jewish peddler in the region—and the one whose name is known to people all over the world into the early twenty-first century—was Levi Strauss, who sold cloth overalls to the men who hoped to strike it rich. Among the few who managed to do so was Strauss, with his "Levis."

Thereafter, Jews have played a continuously important role in San Francisco's civic and economic life. In the nineteenth century, Jews in San Francisco served on all the city's important political boards and commissions. Members of nearly all the influential civic organizations, they held elective office, serving as mayors, judges, city commissioners, county treasurers, regents of the University of California, and representatives to Congress.

Jews were quite prominent in the arts, professions, and in the business sectors. In banking, the Fleishacker and Hellman families, in insurance, J. B. Levison, and in clothing manufacturing and merchandising, I. and J. Magnin joined Levi Strauss and the Neustadter family to form a Jewish elite. In music, journalism, and art, Jewish women and men in San Francisco left their mark on the city. Indeed their legacy can be seen in the many public buildings that bear their names: M. H. de Young Memorial Museum, Sutro Library, Fleishacker Pool. Raphael Weill School, Sigmund Stern Grove, and the Steinhardt Aquarium.

The Jewish contribution and success in San Francisco grew out of the energy the immigrants brought with them, a desire to make their fortunes in California. It also grew out of the newness of the California environment. Everyone in California was a newcomer, with the obvious exception of the native Americans and Mexicans, who had no chance of partaking in the dynamic growth of the city and state. As white people with energy and ambition in a new society without a local elite, Jews were able to rise and become part of the city's upper class.

The later history of San Francisco Jewry includes chapters on the arrival of east European Jews in the early twentieth century, and these people created their own communities and institutions. It also includes the arrival of the Holocaust survivors, who came after World War II. The uniqueness of the Jewish history of this city, however, was shaped by the drama of its first residents.

Opposite: *Rebecca Brodek Harris, who arrived in San Francisco in the early 1850s, with her daughter, granddaughter, and great-granddaughter.*

Right: *Bavarian-born orphan Levi Strauss arrived in San Francisco in 1853 with nothing but a few yards of tent canvas and his native ingenuity. When he noticed the gold miners' rapidly decaying clothing, he had his sturdy canvas fashioned into a dozen pairs of trousers, and sold them all in the blink of an eye. The profits allowed him and his brothers, now organized as Levi Strauss & Co., to procure more canvas and continue innovating, adding blue denim and copper-riveted pockets, and creating a quintessentially American fashion.*

Below: *A Gilded Circle soirée, San Francisco, c. 1890. Left to right, standing: Florence Guggenheim Colman, May Lilienthal Levy, Vera Colman Goss, and name unknown; seated: name unknown, Edith Mack Bransten, Amy Sussman Steinhart. Gilded Circle clans frequently built homes on the same street and often in the same summer retreat. Latter-day architectural heritage buffs would lovingly preserve these beautiful Victorian homes.*

becoming wealthier and found that being Jewish placed limitations on their professional and social lives.

For some, the challenge was too great, and they converted to Christianity. For others, the challenge was how to reform Judaism so that it did not hamper their integration into German society. For the rabbis in Germany, the question was a bit different. How could they revamp Judaism so that educated, affluent young people did not leave their ancestral faith and embrace a Christian denomination?

In America the debate over Reform Judaism went a bit differently. Traditionally, Jewish services had no sermon or music. Worshipers prayed at their own pace. They swayed with the cadences of their own reading. When they finished they walked about, and talked. There was much concern on the part of the reformers, however, about spitting and loud cries and moans. When the congregations decided to introduce mixed seating, music, and weekly sermons—and to emphasize order and decorum—they did so because these changes seemed appropriate to the kind of life they had constructed for themselves in America.

Jewish lay people in America had the freedom to make these kinds of changes for a number of reasons. In new communities there was no existing congregation to resist changes. In the smaller communities that could not support multiple congregations, congregants frequently had to find a middle ground between factions that differed over following established tradition or embracing change. In larger communities, when divisions occurred over reforms, dissident groups broke away to form congregations that followed the ritual practices they preferred. Even moderate-sized communities often had two or three congregations.

In addition, America had very few rabbis during this period. Until 1840, in fact, there were none. As mentioned earlier, lay people did much of the work that rabbis did in Europe, and congregations hired *hazzanim* to chant the service. When they could, they also hired *shochetim*, or slaughterers, to provide kosher meat, and sometimes teachers for their children. At times

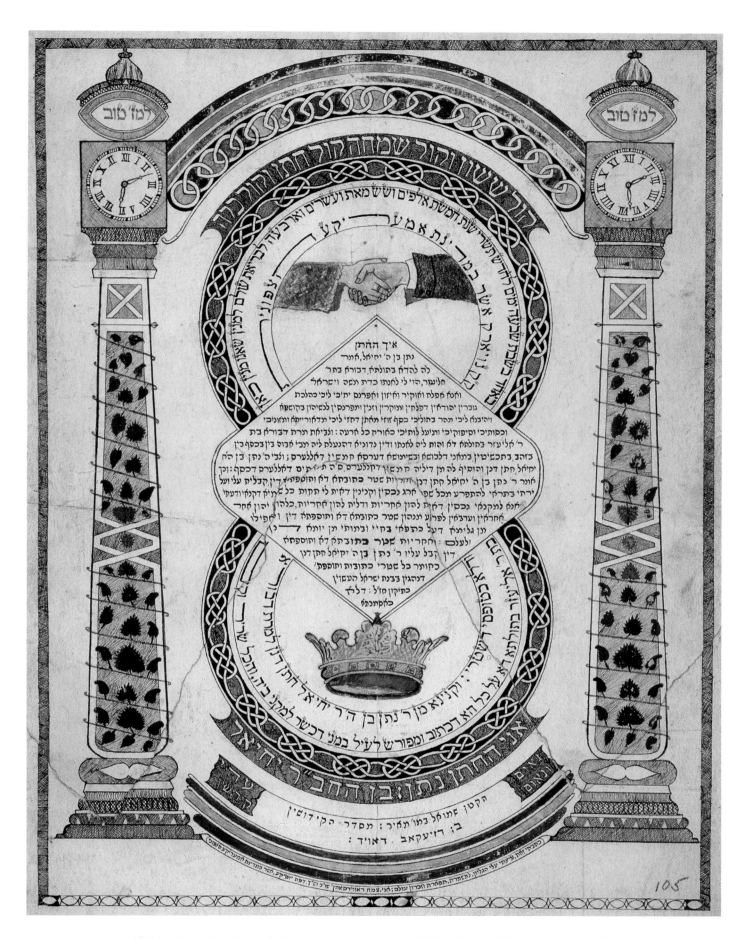

*Ketubbah. c. 1864. Utica, New York. Watercolor and ink on paper. 12 1/2 x 9 1/2 in. The Library of the Jewish
Theological Seminary of America, New York. A grandfather clock sits atop the traditional two columns flanking
a literal depiction, complete with handshake, of the wish for good tidings, "Let it be a propitious hour."
The text in the circles and in the central diamond is the text of the marriage
document for Deborah, daughter of Eliezer, and Nathan, son of Yechiel.*

Hebrew Purim Ball, Academy of Music, New York, March 14, 1865, published in Frank Leslie's Illustrated Newspaper, *April 1, 1865. Like American Jewish life today, earlier Jewish life also enjoyed far wider scope than simply the practice of Judaism at home and in the synagogue. Jewish men and women organized different kinds of associations, including charities for the poor and orphans, literary societies, and fraternal lodges. It is notable that women were as active as men in this regard. No national Jewish organizations emerged until the 20th century. Purim, a late winter holiday observed by costumes and merry-making, was an especially popular occasion for staging fundraisers.*

one person did all these things, and even knew how to perform the craft of *millah*, circumcision.

The first rabbi who came to America was Abraham Rice from Bavaria, who arrived in Baltimore in 1840 to serve the Baltimore Hebrew Congregation. Rice was a strict traditionalist and disliked life in America, where laymen, whom he looked down upon for their lack of piety and learning, made the rules and told him what to do. Rice was correct in that, by and large, American Jews were not particularly observant. Most picked and chose among the commandments of Judaism and observed as they wanted. Some practices, the strict observance of the Sabbath, for example, waned as shopkeepers came to see that Saturday was their biggest day of business. In most of America, stores, by law, had to be closed on Sunday, the Christian holy day. Saturday was the day that farmers and working people bought the goods they needed. For a store to be closed on Saturday meant losing the biggest day of sales.

Other practices were observed, but not meticulously. For example, most Jews wanted to keep *kashrut*, but the smaller and more remote the town, the harder it was. American Jewish newspapers ran advertisements placed by communities and congregations seeking the services of *shochtim*, but it is unlikely that all these positions were filled. In the larger cities—New York, Philadelphia, Baltimore, Boston, Cincinnati—they may have been, and probably most Jews did follow the rules of *kashrut*. But Jews were comfortable, considering themselves loyal and active Jews, even if they did not follow many of the rules of observance at the same time that they considered themselves loyal and active Jews.

While most Jewish social life was built around the Jewish community, Jews were relatively well received by their Christian neighbors. Jews felt increasingly accepted in America, and they did not fear identifying themselves and their institutions conspicuously as Jewish. Synagogues began to have Hebrew words and symbols chiseled or painted on their outside walls. Starting in the 1860s, many congregations built their synagogues in distinctive styles. The most popular style, known as Moorish or Byzantine, looked vaguely Levantine, no doubt alluding to Judaism's roots in the ancient Near East. When synagogues were consecrated, mayors, governors, prominent jurists, and local Christian clergymen attended. Local newspapers covered in detail the dedication of these synagogues and treated the event as good news for the city as a whole.

So well accepted were Jews that when in the 1840s and 1850s a number of anti-immigrant political movements took shape, most notably that of the Know-Nothings, they ignored the Jews. These parties directed their hostility at the Irish in particular and at Catholics in general. That Jews pretty much escaped their venom was testimony to both the high levels of anti-Irish sentiment that engulfed America and the success of Jews in making themselves respectable in the eyes of Americans.

This comfort enjoyed by American Jews led directly into Abraham Rice's final disagreement with his congregation, a disagreement that had a lasting impact on American Judaism. A member of the Baltimore Hebrew

Jewish synagogue, St. Louis, Missouri. The construction of new synagogues and the renovation of old facilities encouraged religious reforms, like mixed seating and the introduction of organ music. Other innovations included shortened Torah readings and observing Jewish festivals for one rather than two days.

Congregation died, and Rice was ready to officiate at the funeral. The congregant had been a Mason. It was not uncommon for middle-class American Jewish men to belong to the Masons, an organization known generally for its fostering of civic goodwill and tolerance.

When Rice arrived at the cemetery, he found that the deceased's Masonic brethren were there, too, expecting to perform their rituals at the graveside. They did not have any problem sharing the services with Rice, but Rabbi Rice had a problem sharing with them. He refused to allow the Masonic ritual to take place in a Jewish cemetery, a piece of consecrated ground.

Several members of the congregation who also were Masons were deeply offended at Rice's actions. They seceded from the Baltimore Hebrew Congregation, and they formed themselves into Har Sinai Verein, becoming the first explicitly Reform congregation in the United States.

In the years after 1840 increasing numbers of American congregations adopted innovations in a kind of piecemeal fashion. Increasingly individual rabbis began to emigrate to America from central Europe. These rabbis, including Isaac Mayer Wise, David Einhorn, Max Lillienthal, Benjamin Szold, Gustav Gottheil, and Solomon Schindler, were much more educated than their congregants. Most of them had been smitten with the ideology of Reform Judaism in Germany, where religious innovators had formed a concrete movement, establishing seminaries to train rabbis and conferences to set the course of reform, publishing journals, and organizing congregations.

Rabbi Abraham Rice of the Baltimore Hebrew Congregation. Arriving in 1840, Rice was the first ordained rabbi in America. His dedication to traditional Judaism alienated a group of congregants, whose reaction was to organize their own congregation, Har Sinai. Lay people were generally much more influential than rabbis in the organization of American Jewish religious life.

In America a complicated relationship emerged between these European rabbis and their American congregants: American congregations had much more control over what the rabbis could do. Rabbis often got into difficulty with members of their congregations, were fired, moved on to new congregations, and once again were involved in controversies with the laymen, who viewed the rabbis as employees.

To these European rabbis, American Judaism seemed chaotic. The rabbis, whether more or less traditional, wanted to impose order. The person most associated in this period with this effort was Isaac Mayer Wise, a rabbi who emigrated from Bohemia in 1846. While there is some question whether Wise was actually a rabbi—that is, if he had really been ordained—he exerted a tremendous influence on the course of American Judaism.

Religion, which for millennia had united Jews, was now, in the modern age and in America, a force that divided them. Congregations split, for exam-

A CLOSER LOOK:
ISAAC MAYER WISE

Considered by many to be the founder of the Reform movement in American Judaism, Wise came to America in 1846 from Bohemia. While there is some question if he ever received rabbinic ordination, Wise arrived in America and was hired as the rabbi of Beth El congregation in Albany, New York.

Wise was infused with the idea that American democracy had the power to transform Judaism. He tried out some of his ideas in Albany at Beth El. Some of the members of the congregation balked at the reforms he was attempting to introduce and after a particularly stormy fracas during Rosh Hashanah services, 1850, Wise's supporters founded a new congregation for him—and his reform schemes—Anshe Emeth.

Here Wise made a radical move. No longer would women sit in a separate section. Rather men and women sat together in family pews. Although the members of Anshe Emeth were untroubled by this innovation, mixed seating would be for many other congregations on the brink of reform a controversial issue.

In 1854 Wise moved to Cincinnati. He was convinced that the future of American Jewry, and America as a whole, lay in the west. Here he became rabbi of B'nai Jeshurun and it was from Cincinnati that he went on to construct the basic apparatus of Reform Judaism in America. He used the two newspapers that he founded, *Israelite* and *S*, as organs by which to disseminate his basic idea: Judaism had to reform itself to fit American conditions and

he was the individual best suited to unite American Jews into a cohesive force.

In 1856, Wise edited a prayer book, entitled *Minhag America*, or the American rite. In 1855 he organized the first rabbinical conference in America, and over the course of the next decades he established the Union of American Hebrew Congregations (1873), founded the first rabbinical training school, Hebrew Union College (1875), which he hoped would ordain rabbis for all movements of Judaism, and in 1889 organized the first organization of American rabbis, the Central Conference of American Rabbis.

Traditionalists, like Isaac Leeser of Philadelphia, argued that Wise had gone too far, that his prayer book tampered with tradition to the point of heresy. More radical reformers like Baltimore's David Einhorn believed that Wise took too moderate a position and that he gave in too much to the traditionalists.

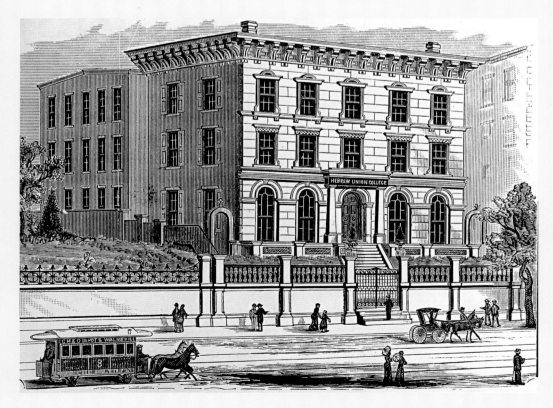

Above: *Isaac Mayer Wise.*
Left: *First Hebrew Union College building, on West Sixth Street in Cincinnati.*

ple, over whether to join the UAHC. Individuals left congregations in anger when boards decided to abandon separate seating or introduce the use of an organ.

But what did hold Jews together was a sense of sharing a common destiny. This union through peoplehood went in three important directions. First, communities large and small recognized that some Jews in their midst were in need: new immigrants, destitute peddlers, fatherless orphans, widows without a male breadwinner, the sick, and the indigent. Jewish communities organized dozens of charitable societies. Obviously, the larger the city, the more complex and formal the charitable network, but in communities large and small, Jews felt the need to take care of each other.

In nineteenth-century America, part of this sense of communal bonding grew out of the threat perceived from Christian missionaries, who made tremendous efforts to convert Jews to what they saw as the one true religion. In hospitals they tried to extract deathbed conversions from Jews. In turn, Jews began to build their own hospitals, so that their sick would be free of this intrusion.

In 1837 in Philadelphia, Rebecca Gratz saw how evangelicals were trying to woo Jewish children toward Christianity. These children, particularly those from poor families, had no formal training in their own tradition, and she considered them particularly vulnerable to the missionaries who roamed the Jewish quarter of the city. She and a number of other women from Congregation Mikveh Israel organized the first Jewish Sunday school, to teach those children whose parents could not afford to educate them. In doing this Gratz created a revolutionary new role for Jewish women: teachers, a position heretofore assumed by men. Gratz, hardly a revolutionary or an adherent of the women's movement then taking shape in America, did what she did because she believed that Jews with means had tremendous obligations toward those without.

Second, Jews in America found common ground as they took upon themselves the cause of their sisters and brothers in other lands. Jews in the

United States, individuals with full political rights, took advantage of their status to lobby on behalf of Jews elsewhere who suffered persecution. In 1840, for example, American Jews held meetings and sent petitions to Congress and to the president on behalf of the Jews in Damascus, Syria, a number of whom had been falsely imprisoned and were being tortured. In the decades to come, American Jews would unite to help Jews in other places around the globe: Switzerland, Italy, Rumania, and Russia. In each one of these episodes, differences in the practice of Judaism faded in the face of common concern with an outside enemy.

Third, sometimes, even in America, Jews needed to band together to combat homegrown persecution and discrimination. While their reactions to acts of hostility were relatively quiet and behind the scenes, they did speak out with a single voice when some of "their own" suffered for the fact of being Jews.

The most dramatic example of this occurred during the U.S. Civil War. Jews had been divided internally on matters of slavery and secession. Generally, southern Jews demonstrated loyalty to their region and its goals, while northern Jews sided with the Union and opposed the institution of slavery. So, too, the rabbis of America split into two factions. Jews fought in the armies of both sides, and Jews on the home front raised money, rolled bandages, and supported the men fighting for the Union or the Confederacy. But two events happened during the Civil War that tested the American Jewish perception of just how thoroughly they had been accepted by their American neighbors.

First, Jewish men who were in the Union Army found out that they could not have rabbis to serve them as chaplains at the front. Because they thought that by this point America had come to accept Judaism as part of religious life, they were stunned when Congress passed an act stating that only ordained Christian ministers could be commissioned in the army. For a year, American Jews lobbied Congress and the president to convince them that Jewish soldiers had spiritual needs and that Judaism should be recognized as a legitimate faith.

The Jewish sense of acceptance was tried further and the Jewish unity heightened when on December 17, 1862, General Ulysses S. Grant, then leading a military department that encompassed northern Mississippi and western Tennessee, issued General Order No.11. In this edict he called for the expulsion within twenty-four hours of all Jews from the region under his command. His argument was that all Jews were involved in trading in contraband and could not be trusted. Jewish newspapers around the country decried this act. Rabbis gave sermons condemning such behavior as alien to the American tradition. The Board of Delegates of American Israelites, which had been founded in 1859 to advocate for Jewish causes, sent letters of protest and organized delegations of Jews who came from all over America to meet with President Abraham Lincoln, urging him to revoke the order. (Lincoln did so immediately upon hearing about it.)

What was emerging in nineteenth-century American Jewry, then, was a community culture that recognized its religious divisions but also the com-

Portrait of Rabbi Bernard Illowy, by Henry Mosler. 1869. Cincinnati. Oil on canvas. 41 1/2 x 31 1/2 in. Gift of the Skirball Foundation. An Orthodox rabbi, Illowy arrived in America in the mid-19th century, during the great influx of Jews from central Europe. This influx helped introduce to the U.S. the reformed model of Judaism championed by the German Reform movement.

Eminent American clergymen. From the American Phrenological Journal, *April 1868 issue. Benjamin Szold, father of Henrietta Szold, the founder of Hadassah, is seen on the bottom left. There were no local Jewish institutions to train rabbis until the 1870s and 1880s. Until then, all Jewish clergy in America either came from or at least were trained in Europe.*

mon destiny, at home and abroad, that held them together. There was a bit of irony in this. Reform Judaism increasingly articulated the position that Jews were purely a religious community, a denomination of Americans like the Methodists or the Presbyterians. For example, when Reform rabbis met in Pittsburgh in 1885, they stated that Judaism was a religious tradition, not a nationality or a people. Yet they, and American Jews, in general behaved quite differently.

Jewish unity would be severely tried in the decades to come. In the 1870s a number of developments began to take shape. Prejudice against Jews seemed to be on the rise. Social clubs, resorts, hotels, and other places of leisure started discriminating against Jews. More Americans, poor farmers as well as upper-class old-stock Americans, began to blame Jews for the ills of

A CLOSER LOOK:
REBECCA GRATZ

The most important nineteenth-century Jewish woman in America, Rebecca Gratz was born in 1781 to Michael and Miriam Gratz of Philadelphia. Rebecca was one of twelve children. As a young woman, she participated in the swirl of social and literary activities that fit elite Philadelphians. She attended balls and literary soirées. She was friendly with Washington Irving, Fanny Kemble, Maria Edgeworth, well-known figures in the Anglo-American literary scene. Her portrait was painted by the distinguished artist Thomas Sully.

Like other wealthy and leisured women of Philadelphia of the early 19th century, Gratz devoted considerable time and energy to philanthropic causes. She helped found several nonsectarian projects like the Female Association for the Relief of Women and Children in Reduced Circumstances as well as the Philadelphia Orphans Asylum. Gratz's work with her Christian peers demonstrated that Jews and Christians could find common ground in service to the community.

By the beginning of the 1820s, large-scale immigration of relatively poor Jews from central Europe began in earnest. As this influx changed the character of America's Jewish communities, Philadelphia included, Gratz turned her attention to Jewish needs and Jewish causes. It was in this that Gratz made her greatest contribution. She conceived of numerous Jewish philanthropic projects, and vastly expanded the role of women within the Jewish community. Gratz demonstrated that in America, new Jewish institutions did not emanate only from the clergy or the synagogues, but from the activities of concerned women and men.

In 1819 she called together the women of Mikveh Israel, her congregation, and together they founded the country's first extrasynagogal charitable society, the Female Hebrew Benevolent Society, intended to alleviate the poverty of Jewish women and children in Philadelphia. Through her stewardship of this society, Gratz was called upon by many sewing societies and fuel societies to help them serve the Jewish poor more effectively.

Women who worked with Gratz in her Hebrew Sunday school then established and staffed similar schools in other communities in America. In order to have more teachers for Philadelphia and the other Jewish communities, Gratz opened a teacher training school, the graduates of which became a powerful educational

Thomas Sully. Rebecca Gratz. *1858. Oil on canvas. 20 x 16 in. American Jewish Historical Society, Waltham, Massachusetts, and New York, New York.*

force elsewhere. In order to teach, Gratz created pedagogic materials, books for students and for teachers. Until that point there were no texts in English for Jewish students and Gratz pointed out that such materials were a desperate communal need.

In the 1850s, Gratz founded the Jewish Foster Home, a place of service to aid Jewish orphans. The structure of the Jewish Foster Home, later renamed the Association for Jewish Children, was copied by Jewish communities all over America, as they struggled with the plight of poor children in the immigrant population.

Above: *Jewish Union soldiers with their southern relatives, Albany, Georgia, c. 1867. In 1861, there were 150,000 Jews in the U.S. While most lived in the north, there were many in the south, where they served in high political office, including in the Confederacy. Jews served in both the Union and Confederate armies, with 7,000 and 3,000 men respectively. Seven Jews won the Congressional Medal of Honor.*

Opposite: *Posen. Schiff Torah Shield (Tas). 1890. Gilded silver, embossed and chased; castings, enameling, lapis, semiprecious stones, niello. 15 3/4 x 11 3/8 in. Courtesy of Congregation Emanu-El of the City of New York. Gift of Jacob H. and Therese Schiff, 1890. Photo: © Malcolm Varon 2000.*

At the same time, the Jewish population of America was growing dramatically. In 1820 there had been about 2,000 Jews in the United States. In 1880 there were 250,000. New Jewish immigrants were flooding to the United States, and the source of that migration began to shift. Jews from eastern Europe—Russia, Poland, Galicia, Lithuania—came in significant numbers to America. Their arrival taxed the charitable institutions of American Jewish life and challenged any emerging consensus of what it meant to be an American Jew.

A GOLDEN LAND
(1870-1924)

etween 1870 and 1924, when the U.S. Congress severely curtailed immigration to the United States, the profile of world Jewry changed dramatically. In 1870 only about two hundred thousand Jews lived in America. Over the course of the next half century, about three million additional Jews arrived, primarily from eastern Europe, transforming America into a major center of Jewish life. This massive population movement had deep implications for the Jews of America, for America itself, and for the subsequent history of the Jewish people wherever they lived.

At the beginning of this era American Jews produced little in the way of books or ideas that Jews elsewhere considered important. It was in Europe, east and west, where great ideas developed, where Jewish books and Jewish institutions flourished.

In 1870, for example, a young American Jewish man who wanted to become a rabbi had to travel to Europe for training. But by the 1920s, rabbis were being ordained in New York and Cincinnati by Orthodox, Reform, and Conservative seminaries, and American Jewish books, newspapers, and plays were making the reverse journey to Europe. By the 1920s, Jews in Europe came to view what American Jews did and said as noteworthy. In international Jewish movements, such as Zionism, which was

Opposite: Alfred Stieglitz. Steerage. 1907. Photograph. Philadelphia Museum of Art, Stieglitz Collection. Gift of Carl Zigrosser. While millions of Jews left eastern Europe for America, not all actually arrived in this country. Some remained in the country of embarkation, Germany, or in a port of call, such as England. Despite the many obstacles facing aspiring immigrants, including difficult conditions of passage, the impetus to leave was still stronger.

born in the 1890s, American votes and beliefs mattered a great deal. And American Jews had more financial resources—and greater political influence—than other Jews.

This change took place because of emigration from eastern Europe. Most of the almost three million Jews who came to America in this period hailed from a broad area east of the Elbe River, a region that by and large was economically less developed than the area to the west, and in which Jews still enjoyed little chance for emancipation and economic comfort.

During the 19th century, most Jews in eastern Europe lived in shtetls, *or Jewish towns, such as this one. Despite the small size of such towns, Jews in eastern Europe were by and large an urban and modern people in comparison to the surrounding populations.*

Jews had been coming to America from eastern Europe for centuries; Polish Jews, Yiddish-speakers, had been present in colonial times. But they had come pretty much as single individuals, not as part of a large-scale migration. The pace of Jewish movement out of eastern Europe picked up in the middle of the nineteenth century. And Jews from Galicia, Lithuania, Poland,

and western Russia joined those from Bavaria, the Rhineland, and Westphalia as peddlers and shopkeepers in America throughout the nineteenth century. However, they, too, had come on their own and not as part of the transformation of their sending communities.

Some of the Russian Jewish young men who came to America in the 1840s and 1850s had left their families and hometowns to evade conscription into the army. This was a fate dreaded by Jews, who were treated mercilessly during their decades-long mandatory service. Moreover, in the late 1860s a number of devastating famines in the western Russian province of Suwalk sent large numbers of Jews to America, the vanguard of the great east European migration that began in earnest in the 1880s.

Another catalyst for emigration were the pogroms, the violent, bloody attacks on Jews that began to happen with frightening regularity in 1881. Organized attacks occurred in the years 1881–1884, 1903–1906, and 1917–1921. Forty-five Jews were brutally murdered in just a few days in Kishinev in April 1903. Local Christians went on these rampages against Jews generally when their own economic conditions were in decline and their own social order was in upheaval. They lashed out against the Jews as

Early-20th-century painting of two refugees carrying wrapped Torah scrolls, escaping after a pogrom in Heimlase, Russia. Although pogroms are a popular reason for explaining the causes of Jewish immigration, greater economic opportunities were more important to Jews than religious freedom.

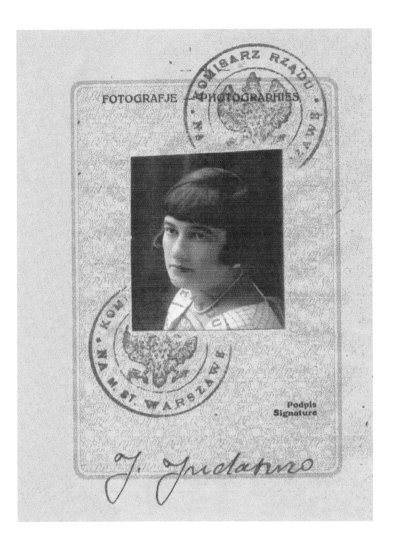

The Polish passport of Jean Judaszko, who emigrated to the U.S. in 1927.

convenient scapegoats, and the political authorities did little, often nothing, to intervene. When pogroms broke out in a region, Jews in the surrounding towns feared for their lives as well, and many began to take seriously the idea of emigrating to America, a place that had already achieved a reputation as a comfortable haven for Jews.

The pogroms were important in spurring the migration, but they were not the only cause. Fundamentally, it was the increased impoverishment of the Jews that made life most difficult in eastern Europe. Jews had been abandoning the small towns, sometimes known as *shtetlach*, of Russia and Poland since the middle of the nineteenth century. Many headed for the big cities of eastern Europe—Vilna, Warsaw, Bialystok, Kiev, Lodz—to find work, since the economic position of the Jews of eastern Europe had worsened with the first intrusions of the railroad into that region. The Jewish birthrate kept going up, however, despite these difficulties and even in the cities, there was not enough work for the petty merchants and artisans who made up the masses of eastern European Jews.

Then in 1882 the May Laws were promulgated in Russia, restricting where Jews could live and what work they could do, which in turn made Jewish poverty even worse. Jews began to think about other places where they might live, where being Jewish was less of a burden. Newspapers, promotional literature, and letters from relatives already in America portrayed the United States as offering a chance to live better and more freely. Thus, Jews in eastern Europe thought of America as a place where they could live without constant hunger and constant fear, where hard work brought a living wage, where Judaism could be practiced unhindered, and where physical violence against Jews was a rarity rather than an everyday threat. Indeed, in sheet music and in common parlance, America was referred to as "Columbus's *Goldene Medine*," Columbus's golden land.

A Jewish cobbler ready for Sabbath Eve in a coal cellar in New York, where he is living with his family, 1887. Photo by Jacob Riis. While the Jewish features of such images catch the eye today, the photographer actually wished to highlight immigrants' poverty.

*Andrew Melrose. New York Harbor and Castle Garden.
1885. Oil on canvas. 22 x 36 in.
The New-York Historical Society. Castle Garden
Immigration Station was the first site of their new home for
many Jewish immigrants who not only landed in but
remained in New York City. It was replaced by the Ellis
Island facility, which opened in 1892.*

For a handful of Jews in these years, the idea of rebuilding a Jewish home-land in Palestine seemed a powerful alternative to pogroms, poverty, and persecution. Thus, the Zionist movement began to take shape in this era. While decades passed before significant numbers of east European Jews decided to build homes for themselves in their once-promised land, those who remained in eastern Europe and those who came to America felt strong sympathies for the movement. They knew all too well what it meant to be a despised people, eternal outsiders never at home.

Unfortunately, many Jews did not find all they'd hoped for in the golden land. And a larger number, in their plight as impoverished workers, thought about ways to transform the larger society. They considered the vastly

The Registry Room at Ellis Island, c. 1900. There are many stories of how officials at Ellis Island changed Jewish family names. In fact, all these officials did was check the information of the new arrivals and make sure that they passed the necessary conditions for immigration.

inequitable distribution of resources to be the cause of anti-Jewish senti-ment. As a result, many Jewish workers and intellectuals in the larger cities turned to socialism as an ideology. In 1897, some formed the Bund, the first Jewish workers' organization. Those who became part of this movement tended to disdain religious orthodoxy. They believed that the restrictions upon Jews imposed by *halachah* and the continuing control of the commu-nities by rabbis had contributed to the impossible situation in which the Jews found themselves.

Among the millions of Jews who came to America after the 1880s, a sig-nificant number had been involved with the Bund or with other Jewish workers' organizations in Europe and held socialist ideas. Once in America, they used those experiences to form unions.

That all lay in the future. Other aspects of Jewish emigration from eastern Europe during this era had some distinctive characteristics. First of all, Jews came to America with no intention of ever going back. In the early years of the east European exodus, a handful did return, but the numbers were

This cartoon from Puck, *1887, depicts Joseph Seligman, a respected Jewish banker, being denied entrance to the Grand Union Hotel in Saratoga, New York, because he was a Jew. In the U.S., anti-Semitism rose in the decades following the Civil War. It was one response to the rapid pace of socioeconomic change, which many felt threatened "Christian" America.*

small. Compared to most immigrants—Italians or Greeks, for example—the Jewish migration to America was permanent. Jews had, after all, really no home to go back to, and they harbored no particularly warm feelings for the places they had left.

Of course, they did continue to be involved with relatives and with the Jewish communities in those towns through their *Landsmanshaftn*, home-town societies that they created in America. Through *Landsmanshaftn,* immigrant Jews in America could send money to friends and family back home, to help them amid the continuing crises they faced. But Jews who made it to America had no interest in going back to those places to resettle.

While most Jewish immigrants, like other immigrants, tended to be young, able-bodied workers, both male and female, a significant number of older people and children made the move as well. About 25 percent of the immigrant Jews were either under fourteen or over forty-five. This tells us that whole families were making the move to America during this era.

It was quite typical for a husband with his older children, sons and daughters, to migrate to America first. Relatives or townspeople already in America would help them find a place to live and jobs, then all members of the family worked and saved their money to send for the rest of the family, the mother and the younger children.

The fact that entire families often came to the United States was one of the other characteristics that made Jewish immigration distinctive. Older people were the repositories of traditional skills and knowledge. They acted as conservators of the past amid the rapid changes that characterized life in this new country. Children, who mingled with other children in the streets and in school, often were the first in their families to learn English and the first to become comfortable outside the insular immigrant enclave.

By the 1870s, the vast majority of immigrating Jews were landing in New York. Of these, most stayed put. In 1905, for example, almost seven hundred thousand Jews lived in New York. The next largest Jewish community was

Chicago, which had about eighty thousand, and then Philadelphia, with seventy-five thousand. Boston was next, with forty-five thousand, and so on, with Jewish immigration being overwhelmingly urban. Trickles of people went to small towns and even to farms to homestead. But well into the middle of the twentieth century, New York continued to be the preeminent American Jewish community.

It was in New York where whole neighborhoods—the Lower East Side in Manhattan, Brownsville and Williamsburg in Brooklyn, Harlem (later on) and sections of the Bronx—took on the flavor of east European Jewish life. Store signs were written in Yiddish, the language of the streets. Yiddish newspapers were available on street corners, as were kosher eating facilities and shops catering to Jewish needs. Yiddish theaters clustered there, particularly in lower Manhattan, as did the *Landsmanshaftn*, synagogues, clubs, lodges, and schools the immigrants founded.

The development of this rich social and cultural life occurred in New York because it was there that east European immigrant Jews found work. They tended to go into two kinds of enterprises, both of which func-

The "New Jerusalem" of New York. This political cartoon, c. 1890s, depicts the fleeing Russian Jews arriving in New York while the older New York families depart for the West. In the center a wealthy Jewish man in top hat holds blueprints labeled "Perseverance and Industry." He stands in the center of Broadway, the buildings of which bear "Jewish" names and occupations. Photo: © Bettmann/CORBIS.

tioned as a kind of Jewish economy. About half went into small-scale business. Some of these businesses were so small that they amounted to nothing more than pushcarts or wheelbarrows on the street, from which the vendors sold odd bits of clothing, foodstuffs, needles, and thread—everyday goods that they marketed mostly to other immigrant Jewish customers. Some operated stores—such as bakeries, groceries, fish markets, clothing shops—ranging in size from tiny to large. Some stores sold goods that satisfied particular Jewish needs: kosher butcher shops, bakeries, cafes

The arrival of Jewish refugee children in the United States, under sponsorship of HIAS, in New York. In 1909, a united HIAS emerged from the amalgamation of two aid societies founded by eastern European immigrants, the Hebrew Sheltering Society (1889) and the Hebrew and Immigrant Aid Society (1902).

and restaurants, and Jewish bookstores. All of these businesses helped many make a living and helped everyone else live a Jewish life in America.

The other half of the immigrant Jewish population, women and men, went into the garment industry, a field of enterprise in which they outnumbered workers of other groups. Needlework was a skill that many Jews in Europe already had acquired, and many had worked in that industry before leaving for America. It was logical that they would seek out garment work in their new home.

Within the garment industry, Jews were not only employees, but also employers: most owners of garment factories were other immigrant Jews. It took relatively little money to open a garment shop, and indeed, some of the smaller garment "factories" were actually just apartments, the same

Boston's North End. The Hebrew characters on the sign to the left indicate that the store is home to a Sofer, *someone who writes and checks Hebrew scrolls, both full Torah scrolls and the smaller scrolls of phylacteries and* mezuzahs.

107

Right: *Hester Street, New York City, c. 1900. Today, Hester Street remains an important landmark of New York's Lower East Side. It was reported that anything and everything could be found on the pushcarts dominating the streetscape in this photograph. For this reason, Hester Street was often referred to as the "chazer market," though* chazer *probably referred to odd assortments of goods, rather than pigs. Non-Jews commented on the remarkable level of activity in the neighborhood, as well as its noise, smells, and tastes. Although pushcarts were an important source of Jewish commerce, most Jews arrived in the U.S. with some kind of trade expertise.*

Below: *"I Cash Clothes," c. 1910. The rag trade, or the* shamata *business, was important for Jews who arrived in the U.S. with no immediate skills or resources. This trade was part of an enormous clothing industry that employed Jews and non-Jews alike. In New York City, the center of this industry before World War I, more than 300,000 workers labored in garment factories and sweatshops, often under terrible conditions.*

Annie Maier (Myers) making Campbell Kids pinafores, New York City, 1911. Photo by Lewis Hine. It was not uncommon for work to be done in private residences or workshops, commonly referred to as sweatshops. Such work offered married women the opportunity to earn a wage while still looking after the home.

space that the boss's family slept and ate in. The workers often had to bring their own machines, and the boss, his wife, and the workers all sewed together. This was the notorious sweatshop, with its horrid working conditions—long hours, a hot and dirty environment, and the sexual harassment of young women. But a worker who saved a bit of money might logically imagine that he could himself become the owner of a sweatshop not unlike the one he worked in.

Pauline Newman, along with Rose Schneiderman, Bessie Abramowitz, and Rose Pesotta, were among the Jewish women who helped shape the American labor movement. They all came to America from eastern Europe, saw the vulnerability of the workers in the garment industry, recognized the dependence of families on the wages of factory women, and took on the responsibility of organizing themselves. In 1901, Newman had come to America with her newly widowed mother and three siblings. At the age of nine, she went to work in a hairbrush factory, and at eleven she entered the garment industry, taking a job at the Triangle Shirtwaist Company.

The Grand Theatre–Jacob Adler in The Broken Hearts. *Photograph. 1903. The Museum of the City of New York, The Byron Collection. Sara and Jacob Adler helped make America, and New York in particular, the heart and soul of Yiddish theater. Leaving Russia when the government banned Yiddish theater as subversive, the Adlers came to New York in the 1880s, where they married and became great stars in Yiddish theater. Sara and Jacob had five children—Frances, Jay, Julia, Stella, and Luther—all of whom became significant figures in the theater. The Yiddish theater was famous not only for its original plays, but also for reinterpreting classic works of drama, including Shakespeare. So, in a Yiddish version of* Hamlet, *set in Russia, Hamlet is a Jewish student and his uncle is a rabbi licensed by the Russian state.*

Right: *Gum vendors and newsboys, Washington, D.C., 1912. While parents wished their children to enjoy the advantages of American education, children's wages could also be critical to family welfare.*

Below: *Newsboy, New Haven, Connecticut, 1909. Photo by Lewis Hine. The social costs of immigration could be high for Jewish families. Many men deserted their wives, and among children delinquency was not uncommon.*

Newman began organizing the workers in her shop even before 1909 and the famous "Uprising of the Twenty Thousand," the first effective industrywide strike in the women's garment industry. Newman inspired the working women on the shop floor, and she also spoke eloquently to affluent women, trying to drum up support for the plight of striking garment workers. She made a sterling reputation for herself in both endeavors, and the newly formed International Ladies Garment Workers Union (ILGWU) hired her as a general organizer.

By the 1910s, due to the tremendous unionization efforts of the ILGWU, which organized those who made women's clothes, and the Amalgamated Clothing Workers, who sewed men's clothes, Jewish immigrant workers did

The famous 4th Street Delicatessen, Philadelphia. Although deli food is now regarded as a quintessentially Jewish food, it was originally particular to German Jews. Most Jews from eastern Europe first consumed it in America.

Opposite: *New York City firefighters answered the call at the Triangle Shirtwaist Factory in 1911. The blaze took 146 lives because of locked doors and missing fire escapes. Right photo: © Underwood & Underwood/CORBIS.*

their stitching and sewing in modern factories, characterized by better pay, better lighting, and less harmful conditions.

Despite improvements, modern factories could still be dangerous. In March 1911 one of New York's most modern garment factories, owned by the Triangle Shirtwaist Company, went up in flames. Still considered the worst industrial accident in American history, the fire claimed the lives of 147 young women, mostly Jewish immigrants, although many were Italian.

The Triangle Shirtwaist fire has an important place in American labor history and American Jewish history. The number of women who perished was high because the employer had locked the doors from the outside and had no fire extinguisher or fire escapes. These shocking facts galvanized public attention and focused it on the need for factory inspection. This fire took place at the height of American Progressivism, an era in which some Americans had begun to demand that the state end its laissez-faire policies and instead intervene to improve conditions for workers and the poor.

Progressives came from many backgrounds, most of them Protestants who attributed their activist political thinking to Christian principles and to the ideals their forebears had brought to the crusade against slavery.

But a sizable handful of the Progressives were Jews, and they came to Progressivism in part through a Jewish journey. For individuals such as Louis Brandeis, Lillian Wald, Julia Richman, Julian Mack, Louis Marshall, Minnie Lowe, and others, a Jewish sense of responsibility toward other Jews shaped their political participation.

Still, the entry into America of almost three million relatively poor east European Jews proved to be something of a crisis for those Jews, immigrant or native-born, who were already in America. The Jews already present had achieved a modicum of comfort and prosperity. Some had done very well; others were experiencing slow but steady upward mobility. They had managed to craft a way of being Jewish in America by transforming themselves into Americans, demonstrating their reliability and respectability, and

A CLOSER LOOK:
SAMUEL GOMPERS

Samuel Gompers shaped the American labor movement. Born of Dutch-Sephardic parents in London, he came to the United States as a teenager in 1863 and went to work in one of New York's many small cigar shops. He joined a local of the Cigar Makers' National Union right away and spent the rest of his life in labor organizing.

In the 1870s his activities focused on the cigar makers' union. He played an active role in its reorganization and stressed the role of the union in improving workers' lives by winning sickness and death benefits for them. His vision of unions focused on such bread-and-butter issues as higher wages and better pay; in exchange, workers would cede much of the control of the union to the national officers.

By the 1880s, Gompers had shifted his attention from the limited scope of the cigar makers' union to the larger world of national labor politics. Without any particular Jewish loyalties, he was instrumental in creating the American Federation of Labor (AFL), an alliance of unions of skilled workers, who were in a better position to demand concessions from employers than the vast majority of American workers, who were unskilled.

Gompers put the interests of the skilled workers at the center of his concerns. In America, he argued, the public at large and employers in particular were hostile to unions. Unions, therefore, should avoid politics because legislatures and courts represented the interests of the employer class. Laborers had no clout in the political arena, so any improvement in their conditions had to come from the strength of their organization and their ability to engage in collective bargaining.

Gompers set out to strengthen the position of those workers he considered most organizable: skilled, white males. He believed that women were unorganizable, and he thought that some immigrants, the poorest and most unskilled, had no place in AFL unions and, as much as possible, should be kept out of America. He saw African American workers as unorganizable as well, and he allowed AFL unions to discriminate against them. Those workers who fit Gompers's model benefitted from AFL policy and from the activities of its craft unions. The majority of American workers did not.

Samuel Gompers, President of the American Federation of Labor,
at a meeting with its executive council, 1924.
Photo: © Bettmann/CORBIS.

embracing reforms in their religious practice that harmonized Judaism with modern American culture.

They were, in a way, then, caught off guard by the massive influx of newcomers. The new arrivals spoke Yiddish, which many already established American Jews may have known, but made a point of not speaking in public. Also, the newcomers settled tightly in certain neighborhoods and, thus, transformed them. Their houses of worship were storefronts, extremely modest structures into which they seemed to have transplanted intact east European orthodoxy. Others spoke on street corners about socialism, anarchism, and other ideologies that seemed inappropriate for America. In the eyes of American Jews, the immigrants were not being sufficiently exposed to American cultural influences.

To complicate matters, the new immigrants inspired much negative reaction from non-Jewish Americans. American writers such as Henry James and Henry Adams wrote with disgust of how American cities, New York

In 1915 the predominantly Jewish Amalgamated Clothing Workers Union went out on strike. Their demands were the abolition of the sweatshop and home work, and a reduction of the twelve-hour work day.

A CLOSER LOOK:
DEPARTMENT STORES

Jews were well-known founders and owners of department stores in New York, such as Bloomingdale's,
Gimbel's, and Lord and Taylor, as well as in other cities
across the U.S., including Boston, Pittsburgh, Memphis,
Dallas, and Phoenix. Most of these business magnates had
emigrated from central Europe and had originally
worked as peddlers.

Above: *Exterior view of R.H. Macy's in New York City, c. 1910.*
Photo: © Bettmann/CORBIS.

Left: *The very successful Mr. and Mrs. Adam Gimbel (of Gimbel's*
Department Store fame) strolling along a fashionable
Palm Beach street. Photo: © Bettmann/CORBIS.

Below, left: *Many of the great department store magnates started*
out as peddlers traveling from town to town in horse-drawn
carriages such as these from Abraham and Straus.

Below, right: *Chicago's Sears Roebuck and Co. had phenomenal*
success with their mammoth mail order catalogue.

and Boston, were being taken over by newly arrived immigrant Jews who were so alien to American culture. Ironically, when elite gentiles evinced anti-Semitic behavior, they tended to take it out on long-established American Jews of means, rather than on the immigrants. Thus immigrant Jews were not touched by the increasing discrimination at resorts and hotels, and they were not particularly affected by the imposition of quotas on Jews at Ivy League colleges and universities. Middle-class Jews with longer roots in American soil were caught between the newly arriving Jews and American Christians who thought that Jews were becoming too numerous and were destroying American institutions.

This group eagerly sought to preserve their relatively comfortable status quo, but at the same time felt a deep sense of responsibility toward the newcomers. They tried various strategies to help the immigrants adjust and to convince non-Jewish Americans that the newcomers would adapt, just as they, the descendants of the earlier Jewish immigrants, had done.

Some among them banded together to protect Jewish political rights and to defend the good name of the Jews. In 1906 some of American Jewry's most notable figures, including Oscar Straus, Cyrus Adler, Louis Marshall,

The Cooper-Levy family from Seattle enjoying a mountain outing. Jews were happy to take advantage of America's vast landscape for holidays. An obvious example is the Catskills in New York State, which became a famous Jewish resort area.

Above: *Julius Meyer, a 19th-century Nebraska trader, meeting with friends and some of his business associates, the Pawnee Indians. Although most Jewish immigrants from central and eastern Europe settled in cities, many were also drawn to more remote areas and the business opportunities they offered. Native Americans sometimes referred to Jewish peddlers as "egg eaters" because they refused to eat meat.*

Right: *Aaron Levy made and lost several fortunes in French Gulch, California; (Russian-owned) Alaska; and Genesee, Idaho, before he and his wife, Esther, finallly settled in Seattle, Washington. Levy and his son-in-law Isaac Cooper founded the Cooper-Levy retail and mail order house in 1892, and the two entrepreneurs made their fortunes selling supplies to gold-seekers in the Alaska gold rush.*

Rose Bros. Fur Co., St. Paul, Minnesota, 1911. The four Rose brothers—Albert, Isaac, Nathan, and Isidore—and James Hill are pictured with Blackfoot Indians. "Two Guns White Calf," whose likeness appeared on the "Indian Head" nickel, stands in front of James Hill. Across North America, Jews were heavily involved in the fur trade. For this reason, they came in contact with peoples who lived on the margins of, or were excluded from, American society, such as Native Americans.

Jacob Schiff, Mayer Sulzberger, and others, formed the American Jewish Committee. They envisioned themselves as an elite body of no more than sixty men who could intercede with American government officials on behalf of Jewish rights abroad and at home.

Two years later some of these same individuals, along with representatives of the immigrant Jewish community in New York, reacted when the city's

Charles M. Strauss and son, c. 1886. Strauss was elected mayor of Tucson, Arizona, in 1883.

Advertisement for Levi Strauss & Co., c. 1899. Levi Strauss came to America from Bavaria in 1847 to work with his two brothers in New York City. Soon after gold was discovered in California in 1849 he went to San Francisco, where he made his mark on the clothing industry with his innovative, durable blue-dyed denim pants. He died a very wealthy man, and left millions of dollars to charities and organizations, both Jewish and non-Jewish.

A CLOSER LOOK:
WOMEN IN THE WESTWARD EXPANSION

Jewish women immigrants often extended their difficult journeys crossing the sea to America with another difficult journey—crossing the plains of America to the even newer world of the American West. Their voices have not often been heard, but recently a selection of nine quilt paintings by Santa Fe artist Andrea Kalinowski, entitled "Stories Untold: Jewish Pioneer Women, 1865–1915," has been formed into an exhibit touring the United States. Devoting as much time to the role of sleuth as that of artist, Ms. Kalinowski has uncovered powerful stories of courage, hardship, and perseverance. Her paintings are virtual tapestries of stories, traditions, and adaptation to a new world woven into the strong structure of authentic American quilt patterns. Excerpts from the pioneer women's stories are offered here with the paintings.

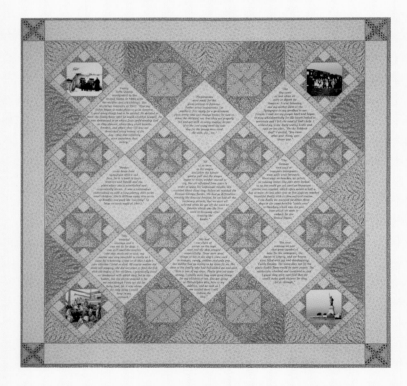

Fanny Jaffe Sharlip immigrated to the United States from Russia in 1889 with her mother and six siblings.

> My father seriously began to make plans to go to America. . . .
> He decided to leave the family home until he could establish himself. He was determined to go where Jews could worship God as they pleased, where they could breathe freedom, and where their life was not threatened every minute of the day . . . that was infinitely more important than money.
>
> We traveled steerage and it was not fit for dogs. I can still smell the terrible odor that made me so sick . . . We had our share of

storms on the high seas and the ship swayed unmercifully. . . . The next morning we saw that great symbol of hope for the immigrants, the Statue of Liberty, and our hearts were filled with joy and thanksgiving. The authorities checked and examined us and I guess they were satisfied that we would make good citizens for they let us through.

Fanny Brooks married at sixteen and sailed immediately to America with her husband Julius. They spent the winter of 1853 in New York and then set out to join a wagon train leaving Illinois for California in June 1854. Fanny Brooks's story is narrated by her daughter Eveline Auerbach:

> They purchased a covered wagon and two little mules, in order to be comfortable; otherwise they would have been compelled to walk. As soon as a sufficient number of wagons could be gotten together, that is a hundred or more, they moved off under their respective captain. He headed the train on horseback with his officers, locating camping grounds and selected crossings over fordable streams, directed construction of rafts for carrying man, beast, and wagon over deep waters. Mother tells that after crossing deep streams they had to take off all their clothing and put on a calico wrapper, hanging their clothes on lines strung from the wheel of one wagon to the wheel of another wagon, and hanging their shoes on the sagebrush to dry. Mother said that often the bottoms of the wagons were filled with water, and clothes and provisions would get wet. After a storm everything was drenched, sagebrush, bunchgrass, and bush. It was almost impossible to make a fire, the smoke would stifle them. Then they had to eat bread, raw bacon, and tea. . . . Mother said they did not suffer as many hardships as the previous trains had suffered as they were better provisioned and had less illness and were not molested by the Indians.

Sarah Thal and her husband homesteaded land in Dodds Township, North Dakota, along the supposed railroad right of way in the spring of 1883.

> That fall my second baby, Jacob, was born. I was attended by a Mrs. Saunders, an English woman. It was in September. The weather turned cold and the wind blew from the north. It found its way through every crack in that poorly built house. I was so cold that during the first night they moved my bed into the living room by the stove and pinned sheets around it to keep the draft out and so I lived through the first childbirth in the prairies. I liked to think that God watched out for us poor lonely women when the stork came.

> In the spring our baby was taken very ill. I wanted a doctor so badly. There was a terrific storm and when it cleared the snow was ten feet deep. My husband could not risk a trip to Larimore. On the fourth day my baby died unattended. I never forgave the prairies for that. He was buried in the lot with Mrs. Seliger and a child of the Mendelson's. For many years we kept up the lonely graves. In time the wolves and elements destroyed them. They are unmarked in all save my memory.

Sophie Trupin, born in Warsaw in 1903, traveled across the ocean in 1908 with her mother and three siblings to join their father in North Dakota.

> After a long voyage across the ocean the journey began all over again, but this time had endless miles of railroad tracks. Somewhere in this vast country was a place called "Nordokota." I had heard that strange name again and again for as long as I could remember. That was where our traveling would come to an end. . . . We traveled all day, and I don't

remember meeting any other wagon or stopping anywhere. There were no houses or trees or rivers, only prairies and hills and sky. To my mother it must have been fearsome and devastating to be plunged into this vast, empty world after knowing only the narrow confines of her familiar ghetto. . . .

My mother kept a kosher home, observing every holiday. This was never easy, but here it was even harder than it had been in the Old Country. There was no kosher meat, and hard-working men needed nourishment, so my father learned how to slaughter fowl in the prescribed way. He had a special ritual knife for this purpose and made a special prayer. I remember seeing my mother making Chanukah candles. I don't know what she used to make them, but they were orange, and I used to look at these candles hanging from the rafters in the woodshed.

The Holy Days were observed with prayers, special dishes which my mother prepared, and cessation from work. However, for the Day of Atonement, Yom Kippur, something special had to be done. Even those Jews who had not spent their Sabbaths in rest and study and contemplation were compelled to stop and remember their training. And so it came about that on the day preceding Yom Kippur all the Jewish homesteaders, who were scattered over many miles, gathered their families and started on a journey to a common meeting place in order to observe the holiest day of the year. The farmhouse that could accommodate the most worshippers was the house of the Weinbergs. It was to be our shul.

From the collection of The Autry Museum of Western Heritage, Los Angeles. Courtesy of Andrea Kalinowski.

In 1892, the city of Denver, Colorado, had only one huppa. *When Ann Korch and Sam Grimes learned that another Jewish couple wanted to marry on the same day they had to coordinate their plans so that both couples could use the only* huppa *in town. Jews settling outside Jewish population centers often faced enormous challenges with respect to traditional observances. However, despite the paucity of Jewish resources, including the absence of clergy, synagogues, and kosher food, Jews still held fast to many Jewish conventions, including the Sabbath and refraining from pork consumption.*

A CLOSER LOOK:
LILLIAN WALD

Born into a middle-class Jewish family in Cincinnati, Lillian Wald made a momentous decision as a young woman when she decided to become a nurse—a relatively unconventional choice for a Jewish woman. Wald's training as a nurse took her into New York's Lower East Side, the densely populated east European Jewish neighborhood, where she saw the harsh conditions in which the immigrants lived. She resolved to bring nursing services and training to them so that they could live in sanitary and healthful conditions despite their poverty. In 1895 she founded the Nurses Settlement on Henry Street, later renamed the Henry Street Settlement. At the settlement house she provided health care, distributed pure milk, and offered neighborhood people educational activities, recreation, and exposure to art and

music. She also created the Visiting Nurses Association, which went into the homes of the poor, bringing medicine, nursing care, and instruction on how to create a healthy living space.

She was part of a remarkable cadre of educated middle-class women of the late nineteenth century who took it upon themselves to better society at a time when the state provided little for the myriad problems associated with immigration and urbanization. She could have settled down to a life of middle-class comfort, but instead she felt a sense of responsibility to the larger community.

Above: *Lillian Wald, nurse and founder in 1895 of the Henry Street Settlement.*

Left: *A Henry Street Settlement nurse goes from rooftop to rooftop to visit homes in order to avoid climbing up and down so many flights of stairs.*

The library of the Educational Alliance, c. 1898. Non-sectarian settlement houses and public libraries were important institutions for immigrant Jews, particularly as sites for acculturation and education. Also, libraries provided space for study, which these Jews, living in tenements and other cramped dwellings, did not otherwise enjoy.

police commissioner, Theodore Bingham, published an article claiming that at least half of New York's criminals were Jews. This led the "uptown" Jews, the American Jewish elite, and those from downtown, the new immigrants, to form themselves into a *kehillah*, the Hebrew term for a formal community. Together the representatives of uptown and downtown would try to stem Jewish criminality, coordinate Jewish education and charity, and to defend the image of Jews in the city.

Others of the elite Jewish group contributed money and expertise to addressing what they considered to be the health and cultural problems of the immigrants. Lillian Wald founded the Visiting Nurses Association and the Henry Street Settlement. Nathan Straus set up milk stations to correct the poor nutrition of the immigrant children. Some set up training schools to teach skills appropriate to the American economy, while still others founded summer camps to get children out of the city into the fresh air.

Jacob Schiff gave the money for what became one of the most influential cultural centers on the Lower East Side, the Educational Alliance.

Right: *Confirmation photo of Henrietta Blum Kempner, 1898, at Temple B'nai Israel, Galveston, Texas. She married I. H. Kempner in 1902.*

Below: *The Solomon family, June 14, 1907, following the marriage of Jacob Weinberger to Blanche Solomon. As noted in the* Arizona Bulletin*: "By reason of the bride having lived here all her life, the event was of more than ordinary interest to the townspeople and the company which witnessed the ceremony included practically all of the American families in the vicinity."*

Throughout the early decades of the twentieth century tens of thousands of immigrant Jewish children took courses at the Educational Alliance, learning art, music, calisthenics, and home economics. It offered practical courses as well. Stenography, typing, and bookkeeping were skills necessary for entry into white-collar work, and the Educational Alliance offered them. It also maintained a Legal Aid Bureau to help immigrants with legal difficulties, and, not surprisingly, it had courses to help them prepare for their citizenship examination.

The National Council of Jewish Women was founded in 1893 by Hannah Solomon. The daughter of earlier immigrants from Germany, she created the organization both to provide direct assistance to Jewish women in need and to lobby state, local, and federal authorities. The council hired agents to track down Jewish men who had deserted their wives, and hired other agents to wait at Ellis Island to meet immigrant girls coming without family and help them find lodging and work.

On the labor front, the unionization of Jewish garment workers was facilitated by American Jews who considered that garment industry strikes hurt Jewish workers, Jewish employers, and all American Jews by extension. In 1910 a bitter cloakmakers' strike was settled through the efforts of Louis Brandeis (who would in a half decade become the first Jew to sit on the U.S. Supreme Court) and Louis Marshall, also a lawyer, and a founder of the American Jewish Committee. They cobbled together a Protocol of Peace, by which the union and the bosses agreed to a set of principles that would govern the industry. Although the protocol lasted only a few years, it created a procedure by which strikes would be resolved.

The effort by American Jews to upgrade the lives of the immigrants extended to the world of Judaism itself. Most immigrants were relatively traditional Jews, and they warmly embraced traditional practice. They felt perfectly comfortable worshiping in small prayer groups, often groups called *anshes* (the word means "people of"), made up of men from the same east European town. Worshiping together was a way to keep Old World friendships alive and to hear familiar melodies.

However, a majority of the children of these new immigrants did not receive a Jewish education. Their families had little money to spend on tuition, and by all accounts, these children had little interest in spending time in the houses of worship their fathers attended. They were well on the road to becoming American, and the ritual practice associated with the *anshes* and other small-scale immigrant institutions did not appeal to them. Even the more substantial immigrant synagogues, such as the Eldridge Street Synagogue, dedicated on Manhattan's Lower East Side in 1887, did not inspire much in the way of active attendance on the part of American Jewish children. If they attended, they did so to fulfill family obligations, and not out of a commitment to Judaism.

The synagogue and Jewish practice had to compete with other influences that were shaping the identity of the next generation. These American youngsters, products of immigrant homes, were comfortable in the streets of their neighborhoods. They enjoyed American popular culture: nickelodeons, silent movies, baseball, amusement parks. American schools also had a considerable impact on them. They saw education as the way to a

A Russian refugee boy takes a violin lesson from his instructor, at Hull House, Illinois, 1910. Photo by Lewis Hine. Settlement houses offered a wide range of classes, instruction, and lectures. Their strong focus on cultural activities helped introduce many immigrants to art, music, and literature.

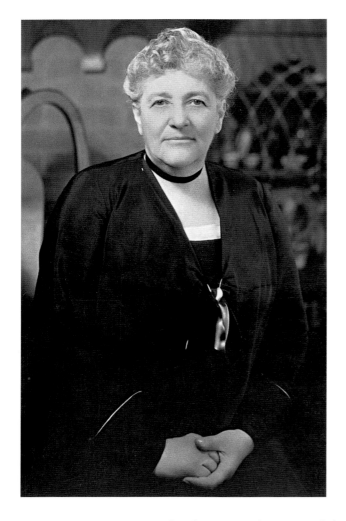

Florence Prag Kahn was the first Jewish woman to serve in the United States Congress. After her husband, Congressman Julius Kahn, died in office in 1924 she stood for a special election and won. She proceeded to win election five times based on her outstanding service to her San Francisco constituents. An able legislator, she authored numerous bills for the development of the Bay Area, and in 1930 was appointed to the Military Affairs Committee, the first woman to serve in that powerful position. Throughout her life Florence Prag Kahn maintained her connection to the Jewish community as well, as an active member of the National Council of Jewish Women and Hadassah.

better life, an avenue toward mobility. Some—both girls and boys—applied themselves to learning with the kind of intellectual zeal that in Europe had gone toward the study of Jewish texts. In America, however, they immersed themselves in mathematics, science, history, and world literature.

Socialism also competed with Judaism for young Jews' attention. A sizable number of socialists and other radicals flamboyantly eschewed Judaism as a religious system. Some even overtly demonstrated their disdain for Jewish tradition. On the Lower East Side, for example, anarchists staged a yearly Yom Kippur Ball, a bacchanalian feast of dancing, eating, and drinking on the eve of the holy day of the Jewish calendar that was traditionally set aside for fasting and prayer.

On the other side, a group of lay people and rabbis fretted over the religious lives of the young people. They asserted that the traditionalists were not doing enough to keep their American-born children part of the Jewish fold and that the antireligious element was providing an attractive alternative to Judaism. They believed that American culture, the kind that immigrant children were discovering on the streets, corroded Jewish loyalty. They also understood that Reform Judaism held little attraction for these children of east European families. It was too formal, and too concerned with decorum to speak to them.

This group founded the Jewish Theological Seminary in New York in 1886. The seminary, which started very small, was to produce rabbis comfortable with the English language and American culture and at the same time knew the Jewish sources. The seminary was conceived as an orthodox institution that embraced American culture, one that remained true to the idea of Jewish tradition and law, but in the context of modern scholarship.

Most of its early students came from the immigrant community, the sons of east European Jews now in America. And the seminary struggled with its funding in order to provide rabbis to help guide the east European Jewish congregations forming in America.

The Jewish Theological Seminary did not initially see itself as creating a new denomination or movement in America. But when in 1902 wealthy American Jews such as Louis Marshall provided money to rescue the school, they insisted that the school bring from Cambridge a renowned scholar, Solomon Schechter, to be its head. In 1913 Schechter and the graduates of the seminary formed themselves into the United Synagogue. Through this organization they helped define a new entity in American Judaism, the Conservative movement.

Born in Rumania in 1847, Solomon Schechter came to the United States in 1902 and became president of the Jewish Theological Seminary of America. Due to his efforts, Conservative Judaism became one of the two major denominations in American Judaism.

So the more economically secure American Jews did much for the newer arrivals, but the immigrants shaped much of their own lives as well. They established their own unions and other workers' organizations such as the Arbeiter Ring, or Workman's Circle. They created resorts and summer camps for their leisure time. They flocked to the Yiddish theaters, which were clustered in New York, with some in Philadelphia, Chicago, and other cities. They created orphanages, old-age homes, day nurseries, medical clinics, and other social service agencies.

Few institutions were as important in the evolution of their culture in America as the Yiddish press. Hundreds of Yiddish newspapers circulated in America. Many were published only briefly and soon died out. Some served the Yiddish speakers of particular cities—Boston, Cleveland, Philadelphia,

Chicago, and Milwaukee: all had their own daily Yiddish papers. All of them mixed news specific to the concerns of Jews with the major stories of interest to all Americans. In the Yiddish newspapers one could read short stories and excerpts of novels, reviews of Yiddish plays, advice columns, cooking columns, and advertisements for goods and services, all written in Yiddish. An important section of the newspapers were the want ads, a good source of information for job seekers and apartment hunters.

The lynching of Leo Frank, near Fry's Gin, two miles from Marietta, Georgia, August 17, 1915. After his conviction, Frank's sentence was commuted from the death penalty to life imprisonment. Unhappy, local Georgians formed a lynch mob, abducting Frank from the Atlanta Penitentiary. Photo: © Underwood & Underwood/CORBIS

The most important Yiddish newspaper in America, the *Forverts*, sometimes known as the *Forward* or the *Jewish Daily Forward*, in 1916 sold almost two hundred thousand copies a day in New York. It published twelve out-of-town editions for Jews in other cities. Its editor, Abraham Cahan, made himself and his newspaper a force in the lives of the immigrants, helping to shape their politics, their cultural lives, and the course of unionization. The *Forverts* ran a very popular and lively advice column, "The Bintel Brief." Readers wrote in with questions about their love lives, problems with their children,

religious questions, and political questions, and the column published many of them, offering readers then—and now—an intimate look into the immigration experience.

The story of this era was the story of immigration from eastern Europe and settlement in America. It was the story of Jews rebuilding old institutions in a new home and creating new ones from the ground up.

But this story was also the story of the American-born children of these immigrants confronting American opportunities and challenges. The children who came to America young or who were born in the United States took advantage of American educational experiences. By the 1920s, the daughters of immigrants were flooding the field of schoolteaching in New York. Many of their sons were moving into the professions of law and medicine, as well as ascending in the world of business. Few of the children followed their parents into garment shops or open-air pushcart markets.

Some of these young people became important figures in American popular culture. Eddie Cantor, Sophie Tucker, Al Jolson, Fannie Brice, George and Ira Gershwin, Aaron Copland, George Jessel, Benny Goodman, and Gus Kahn all had immigrant parents. All had lived in east European Jewish immigrant neighborhoods, and all entertained Americans in the American's own language, as did the Jews who went to Hollywood in the early decades

Above, left: *Yiddish film poster, c. 1930. The Yiddish film industry produced many films in the United States during the 1930s and 1940s. Ludwig Satz was one of the most recognizable actors in the business and appeared in the first Yiddish talking picture.*

Above, right: *Yiddish theater poster, c. 1920. The Yiddish theater was one of the most popular forms of entertainment for newly arrived immigrants.*

of the century. The movies, theater, and music they helped shape were distinctively American.

However, the comfort the immigrants and their children increasingly felt in America was not total. It was complicated in two directions.

On the one hand, the period of the great east European Jewish immigration culminated in a high point of American anti-Semitism in the 1910s and the 1920s. In that decade, Leo Frank, a young Jewish man in Atlanta, Georgia, was brutally lynched, having been falsely convicted of murdering a young girl. In the wake of Frank's blatantly trumped-up arrest and conviction, the B'nai B'rith founded the Anti-Defamation League (ADL), an organization dedicated to ferreting out anti-Semitism in American society.

But the ADL could only do so much. Even after it was founded, acts of anti-Semitism caused many American Jews—new immigrants, their children, and the descendants of earlier-arrived Jews alike—to feel a great deal of anxiety. Colleges and universities began to restrict the number of Jews they would admit. Law firms and hospitals discriminated against Jewish attorneys and physicians. Even the telephone companies in cities such as Boston and New York refused to hire Jews as operators.

Anti-Jewish magaziness and books circulated throughout America. Many claimed that major Jewish figures in the American movie industry were subverting American values. Others accused Jews of being revolutionaries or Communists. This was a powerful accusation in the aftermath of the Russian Revolution. Other publications claimed that Jewish bankers and financiers were sucking the lifeblood out of good Christian Americans.

The rise in anti-Semitism in America, which became more pronounced in the 1920s, might be best illustrated by the experience of Louis

Sadie Ruskin and her wedding party followed the fashion of the day when she married Dory Hornstein in New Jersey, c. 1920.

Brandeis. A Harvard-educated lawyer, he was a hero to American Progressives, having argued several notable cases before the Supreme Court. In 1916 President Woodrow Wilson nominated Brandeis to the Supreme Court.

The naming of Brandeis unleashed a torrent of heated discussion. Many jurists protested. They believed it inappropriate for a Jew to sit on the

Food Will Win the War.
c. 1918. This poster written in Yiddish was also published in several other languages by the U.S. Food Administration. To reach Jewish consumers, American companies advertised in the Yiddish press. Sensitive to Jewish dietary laws, food producers offered reassurances about the purity of their products.

Supreme Court of a nation that was by majority Christian. One letter that came to the Senate said that Brandeis "is a Hebrew, and therefore, of Oriental race and his mind is an Oriental mind, and I think it very probable that some of his ideas . . . might not be the same as those of a man possessing an Anglo-Saxon mind." It took the Senate months to deliberate, and the appointment barely squeaked through.

American Jews exposed anti-Semitism as best they could. They shied away from institutions that discriminated against them, instead founding their own hospitals and law firms. But they proved powerless against the most significant manifestation of anti-Semitic and anti-immigrant sentiment in America. By the early 1920s, that hostility had reached such a high level that Congress ended free and open immigration to the United States, cutting off the possibility that the Jewish population in America would ever again grow substantially through the arrival of newcomers.

This was a great blow to American Jews. Since most were either immigrants or the children of immigrants, they still had family in eastern Europe—sisters and brothers, parents, aunts and uncles, or childhood friends who still lived in Russia (now the Soviet Union), Poland, or Rumania. Under ordinary circumstances this might not have been a problem; they could obviously still communicate by mail, and under the right conditions, American Jews could make return visits to see their east European kin.

Jewish merchants used Jewish images and symbols in their advertising to attract Jewish customers. Other hallmarks of Jewish commercial life included the practice of shopping on the Sabbath, as well as shopping in "honor" of holidays, such as Hanukkah and Passover.

But these were no ordinary times. In the aftermath of World War I and the renegotiations of geopolitical borders in eastern Europe, Jewish life became even more dangerous and problematic than before.

Poland and the crisis of its Jews provides a good example. Until the end of World War I, no such independent country existed. Poland had been carved up among Germany, Russia, and Austria-Hungary in the late eighteenth century. The Treaty of Versailles, which ended the war, created Poland. Nationalism ran high in the new nation. So did economic insecurity. This proved to be a lethal combination for Poland's most visible group of "outsiders," the Jews. Boycotts of Jewish stores, pogroms, and discrimination against Jews took place in the cities and towns of Poland in the 1920s. Poland's enormous Jewish population, numbering into the millions, lived in in a state of constant fear.

American Jews as individuals and through their organizations contributed vast amounts of money to sustain their relatives back home. As long as immigration was an option, Jews in America urged their family members and friends to join them. The ending of immigration changed all that.

For American Jews in 1924, life in America was good. They found themselves well set on the road toward fulfilling, for themselves and their children, the expectations they had brought with them. The anti-Semitism that existed in America bothered them greatly, but it was far outweighed by the community life they had created, the opportunities they could take advantage of, and the knowledge of how much worse Jewish life was elsewhere.

A CLOSER LOOK:
LOUIS BRANDEIS

Louisville-born and Harvard-educated, Louis Brandeis was the first Jew to sit on the United States Supreme Court. His journey to the highest court in the land reveals much about both America and the status of Jews within its borders. After graduating from Harvard Law School in 1877, Brandeis spent his legal career representing the interests of ordinary people against the emerging corporations. In Boston, where he practiced, he became known as the "people's attorney" for his advocacy on behalf of consumers. He also developed the notion that sociological evidence should be admissible in court. Dubbed the "Brandeis brief," this line of reasoning was used, often successfully, to argue for the rights of workers, women, children, and others who lacked obvious protection against corporate interests. In 1911 he was one of a number of notable American Jews who helped mediate an unprecedented strike of the garment industry's cutters and pressers that had pitted Jewish immigrant laborers against Jewish employers.

Brandeis's legal style attracted the attention of President Woodrow Wilson, who nominated Brandeis to a vacancy on the Supreme Court in 1916. This unconventional nomination of both a Jew and an outspoken critic of corporate power led to a vitriolic debate that lasted for months. Many in the Senate and around the country believed that a Jew should not occupy a position of such importance in America, and the Senate only narrowly approved his nomination in June 1916.

Louis D. Brandeis, labor lawyer and U.S. Supreme Court justice.

As a jurist, Brandeis continued to chip away at the vast powers that Congress and the Court had given to corporations. He endorsed the idea that the minimum wage, price controls, and trade unions were constitutional. He also asserted that the federal government had to protect freedom of expression.

Brandeis was an important figure in American Zionism. He came to Zionism in part through his mediation work in the garment industry and his exposure to the east European immigrant Jewish community. In 1914 he became chairman of an important American Zionist body, the Provisional Committee for General

Zionist Affairs, and his close relationship with Woodrow Wilson played a part in the British decision to issue the Balfour Declaration in 1917, which endorsed the idea of a Jewish homeland in Palestine.

Despite much bickering within the Zionist movement, Brandeis remained a steadfast supporter of its cause. He helped organize various economic projects for the small Jewish settlements in Palestine, and in his will he left most of his money to further the Zionist enterprise.

Below: *Chambers Steet Shul, West End, Boston. The* bimah *was built by Sam Katz in 1920. Unlike traditional synagogues in eastern Europe, American synagogues tended to place the* bimah, *the pulpit, at the front rather than in the middle of the building.*

Right: *The Freund family reunion, c. 1920, illustrates the level of acculturation that many Jewish families had achieved by the 1920s. Several of the men and women have retained their traditional appearance, while others have adopted the look of their contemporaries in America. Among Jewish immigrants, the pace of acculturation was swift, especially for children. Bridging generational gaps within families was a major challenge for American Jewish life.*

Jewish refugee children, enroute to Philadelphia aboard the liner President Harding, *waving at the Statue of Liberty, 1939. Despite the relatively small number of German Jews admitted to the U.S. after the Nazis came to power in 1933, they have had a remarkable impact on American cultural and intellectual life, contributing significantly to the arts, humanities, social sciences, and sciences.*

HOPE AND DESTRUCTION, AT HOME AND ABROAD (1924–1948)

In the years spanning the two world wars, Jewish women and men in America underwent a profound internal transformation. At the beginning of this era, the majority of the Jewish population were immigrants, but by the end of the period, those born in America outnumbered those of foreign birth. This was not a simple demographic transition. Immigrant Jews had been notable for their initial foreignness, for their need to learn American ways, for the differences between themselves and other Americans. Their children were a new breed. Not only could they list the United States as their birthplace on forms and applications, but they spoke English with utter ease and unlike many of their parents knew how to participate in American institutions.

After the passage of immigration restrictions in 1924, few new Jewish immigrants came to America. In the late 1930s and early 1940s, American Jews talked about the need to lift the immigration quota as a temporary measure so that Jews could escape the danger of the Nazis. But the 150,000 who did make it to the United States represented just a small fraction of the European Jewish population, six million of whom were killed.

The story of the German Jewish refugees was a painful one. Many were highly trained, well-educated professionals who could not replicate in

HELP RESCUE THROUGH EMIGRATION **HELP**

שיפען מיט גערֵאטעװועטע דורך האַיֵאַס
קומען צו אונזערע ברענען!

העלפֵט זיי קומען

וױיזט אײער דערבֵארמונג הײנט

העלפֵט **האַיֵאַם** העלפֵט

אין דער הייליגער רעטוונגם ארבעט

שנדֵר׳ֵט פֵֵאר האַיֵאַם

CONTRIBUTE TO HIAS

HEBREW SHELTERING and IMMIGRANT AID SOCIETY
10 TREMONT STREET, BOSTON, MASS.

Above: HIAS poster. After World War I and with new immigration restrictions, HIAS's mission changed from helping new immigrants to assisting Jewish refugees and displaced persons abroad.

America the comfortable lives they had once lived. Jewish organizations such as the Jewish Joint Distribution Committee and the Hebrew Immigrant Aid Society tried to help find them homes and work. Local Jewish charitable societies and Jewish community councils took up refugee work as an important task, and social workers and volunteers attempted to ease the strain endured by these people who had been forced out of their homeland.

Most German Jewish refugees chose to settle close to each other, in neighborhoods where they tried to re-create the feel of German culture. In places such as Washington Heights, in upper Manhattan, they opened shops that sold familiar food, and they created synagogues where the German language could be heard. They carved out new lives for themselves, but few of them recouped the professional status and affluent lifestyle they'd had in Germany. Their numbers were also too small to make an impact on American Jewish social patterns.

After the 1920s, the number of Jews in the United States never grew again. The freeze on immigration was only one cause. The other was that American Jews, eager to achieve middle-class status, opted for small families, much smaller than those of other working-class Americans. Jewish women and men chose to limit their families to two or at the most three children. With small families, they believed, they could invest in their children's education and ensure the kind of material acquisitions that would make life more comfortable.

At the beginning of the period, Jews also improved their work and living conditions outside the Jewish communities. By the end of the era, most of them had moved, several times, away from the areas of first settlement, the old slum areas of the immigrant generation. The Lower East Side, the original Jewish immigrant neighborhood in New York, began to lose Jewish population as early as the second decade of the twentieth century. Jews leapfrogged out of the Lower East Side and equivalent neighborhoods in Chicago, Boston, Baltimore, Cleveland, and Philadelphia in every decade.

With each move, they got farther and farther away from the old neighborhood and found larger, airier apartments or even single-family houses with lawns—residences that conveyed a feeling of privacy and family self-suffi-

Choir grouped around the cantor at a celebration of Shevouth at Congregation Chai Odom, in the Dorchester neighborhood of Boston, 1939. Choirs became popular in Orthodox congregations, as well as in Reform and Conservative congregations. They were thought to aesthetically enhance the Jewish prayer service.

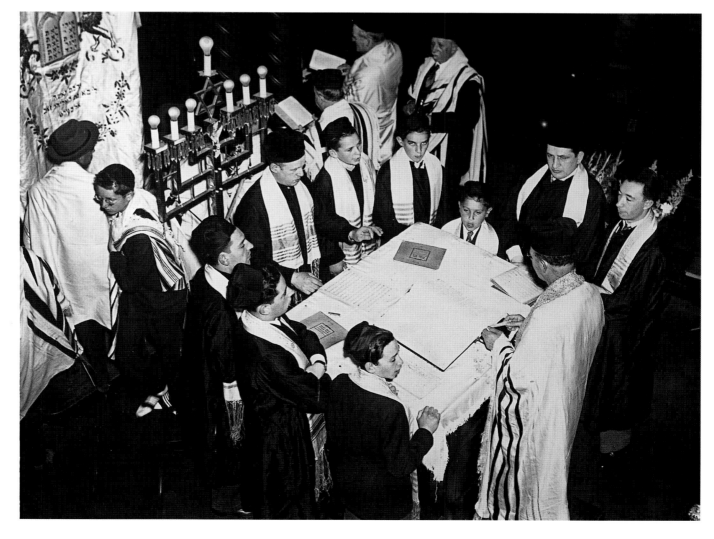

ciency. Until the 1920s, every time Jews moved out of a neighborhood, new Jewish immigrants had come in and taken their places. Once immigration was halted, their places were taken by other newcomers to American cities, not Jews. In many cities African Americans from the South, participants in the northward migration, opted for the neighborhoods Jews were in the process of leaving. For years there was some overlap between the Jewish and the African American communities. The encounter between these two groups in New York's Harlem, Chicago's South Side, and Boston's Dorchester and Roxbury neighborhoods was complicated and led to tensions that affected both communities.

In the years from the 1920s through the end of the 1940s, Jews were capable of this geographic mobility because of their upward economic mobility. No immigrant group in America moved upward on the economic scale as rapidly as the Jews. Fewer and fewer of them worked in garment factories. Instead, relying heavily on educational opportunities, many moved into the professions. By the mid-twentieth century, 20 percent of the men were professionals, double the national average. In New York, where over half of American Jews lived, Jewish women starting in the 1920s flooded the ranks of the city's schoolteachers. These young women took advantage of the free public education available at Hunter College. Those who did not choose schoolteaching often decided on social work or librarianship. A handful defied the usual gender barriers and pursued law and medicine, fields that so many of their brothers were entering, having received their education at the City College of New York.

Not all young Jews in these years went to college. Opportunities in business made it possible for many to afford better housing in neighborhoods nicer than the ones they had grown up in. But whether the route was through education into the professions or through business, this was a period that saw the transformation of the Jews into a stable part of the American middle class.

Some Jews in this period did extremely well. A remarkably visible group of them operated in Hollywood and in other sectors of the American enter-

A CLOSER LOOK:
MEDIA

From radio and television to journalism, Jewish Americans have played a pivotal role in the dissemination of information to the American public. Russian-Jewish immigrant David Sarnoff was instrumental in developing and refining the technology necessary to send radio waves over the air. He became general manager of the Radio Corporation of America, the first significant American radio network, in 1921. It later became NBC.

William Paley became president of Columbia Broadcasting System after purchasing half the network in 1928. He was the first to highlight news reporting in radio programming. Sports reporting came to radio through the colorful baseball broadcasts of Mel Allen, who became the voice of the New York Yankees.

Joseph Pulitzer, creator of the prestigious Pulitzer Prize for achievement in journalism and letters, changed the newspaper business drastically when he bought the *St. Louis Post-Dispatch* in 1878, and offered never-before-seen features in a major daily newspaper—women's fashion, sports, and comics, among others.

Right: *David Sarnoff. Photo: ©Bettmann/CORBIS.*

Below, left: *William Paley.*

Below, right: *Joseph Pulitzer.*

Al Jolson is caught between the old life, a temple macher *(on the left), and the new, his girl Mary (on the right) in* The Jazz Singer, *1927. The Museum of Modern Art/Film Stills Archive.*

tainment industry. Jews such as Jerome Kern, Oscar Hammerstein, and others helped create the theatrical musical as a widely popular American art form, and most of the movie industry moguls were Jewish. Louis B. Mayer, Adolph Zukor, the Warner brothers, and Harry Cohn were among those who defined the film industry.

As screenwriters, actors, producers, directors, owners of movie studios, and operators of movie theaters, Jews helped define American culture. Most of the movies they made depicted America as a relatively happy place where obstacles could be overcome and every drama had a happy ending.

Only occasionally did Jewish topics show up in the movies. *The Jazz Singer,* made in 1927, was an interesting exception. Inspired by a 1922 short story, "The Day of Atonement," this first talking motion picture told the story of a young man—played by Al Jolson—who decided to abandon the tradition represented by his father, a cantor, for a life in show business. The film's happy ending, in which he returned, a great success, to his father's synagogue to chant the Yom Kippur liturgy, told American Jews of this era that they could be thoroughly successful Americans and Jews as well.

In these years, an elaborate New York Jewish culture of summer leisure in the Catskill Mountains came into being. From simple bungalow colonies known as *kochaleins*—"cooking by yourself"—to elaborate resorts such as Grossinger's and the Concord, American Jews pursued pleasure in the country, mixing with other Jews, eating Jewish-style food, and enjoying the entertainment that made the "Borscht Belt" famous.

In the very middle of this era were the difficult years of the 1930s. Like all Americans, Jews were affected by the crisis of the American economy. Many struggled with unemployment or underemployment. Among the unemployed, old practices from the era of immigration came back. Families doubled up, sharing space. They returned to the diet of their early years in America, with lots of soups and potatoes and much less meat. Some of the old social problems that seemed to have vanished with the rise of an American generation also came back, and Jewish social work agencies once again worried about the impact of poverty on family stability.

Jewish charities geared up to ease the burden of the Depression. Jewish communities had within them, ready to spring into action, social service agencies staffed by trained social workers. Jewish voluntary associations also helped Jews facing empty larders or empty bank accounts. Those Jews with means understood that it was their responsibility to help other Jews in moments of distress, just as Jews had done for centuries.

Sometimes this was not enough, and occasionally Jews ended up taking public assistance. Still, in studies conducted during the 1930s, Jews, unlike most other Americans, did not blame themselves for their lack of jobs. Most other Americans tended to internalize responsibility, whereas Jews, when questioned by relief workers, blamed the economy and the American system by which resources were distributed. And they took action. In New York and other large Jewish communities, Jewish housewives protested noisily in the streets against high food prices at a time when so many families had scant resources.

A CLOSER LOOK:
COMPOSERS FOR STAGE AND FILM

The music written by American Jewish composers is a virtual treasure trove of well-worn American classics, including such favorites as *An American in Paris* and *Porgy and Bess* by George and Ira Gershwin, *Guys and Dolls* by Frank Loesser, *My Fair Lady* by Alan Lerner and Frederick Loewe, *West Side Story* by Leonard Bernstein and Stephen Sondheim, *Appalachian Spring* and *Fanfare for the Common Man* by Aaron Copland, and *Company* and *Follies* by Stephen Sondheim. The list could go on and on.

Born Israel Baline in Kirghizia, Russia, Irving Berlin composed such classic American songs as "God Bless America," "Alexander's Ragtime Band," and over a thousand others. The son of a cantor, he came to America as a youngster in 1893 and started in show business as a singing waiter. Despite the lack of any formal musical training—he never could read music—Berlin went on to write the music for such popular Broadway shows as *Annie Get Your Gun* (1948) and *Call Me Madam* (1950) and Hollywood films as *Top Hat* (1935), *On the Avenue* (1937), and *Holiday Inn* (1942).

Showboat, *Sweet Adeline*, *The Cat and the Fiddle*, and *Roberta* were only four of the musical productions composed by Jerome Kern. *Showboat* may have been the most popular and enduring, but during his career he wrote more than a thousand songs for 104 stage shows and films, and some of his tunes, such as "Smoke Gets in Your Eyes," have entered into the canon of American popular music. Kern was born in New York in 1885 to a comfortable middle-class Jewish family. He published his first song, "At the Casino," in 1902, when he was seventeen years old.

George Gershwin was born Jacob Gershovitz, the son of Russian immigrant Jewish parents. He dropped out of high school to take his first job, at a music publishing firm, and by the age of twenty-one was known in the world of New York theater as a pianist. He composed scores for sixteen shows between 1919 and 1925, joined by his older brother Ira as a lyricist. Gershwin later turned his attention to "serious" classical music, achieving such successes as *Rhapsody in Blue* and the full-length opera *Porgy and Bess*.

Opposite: *The Ziegfeld Theatre production of Jerome Kern's classic,* Showboat (1927), *in 1946.*

Right: *Irving Berlin on stage in 1942 performing his song, "Oh How I Hate to Get Up in The Morning," which he wrote for the musical comedy* This is The Army.

Above, left: *George Gershwin making a change to the score for* Porgy and Bess, *1935.*

Above, right: *Jerome Kern chats with actress Jean Harlow, who is going to perform his first motion picture composition in* Reckless, *1935.*

A CLOSER LOOK:
HOLLYWOOD

It is one of the great ironies of American life that the dominant images of America in the mass consciousness were created by Hollywood, and Hollywood, in a profound sense, was created by immigrant Jews from eastern Europe. In the early 1900s, the nascent motion picture industry was taken over, and transformed, by the likes of Adolph Zukor, Carl Laemmle, Samuel Goldwyn, Louis B. Mayer, Harry Cohn, William Fox, and the Warner brothers (Harry, Albert, Sam, and Jack).

Zukor, a Hungarian immigrant, staged a hostile takeover of Paramount, and ran that studio for decades. His pioneering, visionary ideas about the unexplored possibilities of feature films expanded *everyone's* awareness of what could be done in the medium. German-born Laemmle founded Universal Studios, the largest movie studio of its time, in 1912. Goldwyn, among the first to hire important authors such as Sinclair Lewis and Lillian Hellman to write screenplays, was born Schmuel Gelbfisz in Warsaw. His Goldwyn Pictures eventually became part of Metro-Goldwyn-Mayer (MGM), under the leadership of Louis (born Eliezer) Mayer. Mayer, who ran MGM with a paternalistic hand and an obsessive desire for the appearance of sophistication, was probably the most famous of all the film moguls in his time, and his was certainly the largest and wealthiest studio. The Warners, a Yiddish-speaking family of Polish Jews, started out as theater owners, moved into film distribution in search of greater profits, and

eventually decided that producing films made more sense than buying and reselling them. Their first two films failed totally, but their luck turned around soon enough, and their studio became a huge success.

Ever since, although Jews have made up a small percentage of America's population, they have controlled more than half of the power positions in Hollywood. Executives such as Sherry Lansing of Paramount, Harvey Weinstein of Miramax, and Disney's Michael Eisner run things behind the scenes, while prominent Jewish artists—including Stephen Spielberg, Stanley Kubrick, the Marx Brothers, Mel Brooks, Neil Simon, Woody Allen, and Billy Crystal—have always been able to appeal to mainstream tastes, while still finding small and not-so-small ways for their Jewish heritage and perspective to color their films.

Below: *The Warner brothers (left to right): Sam, Harry, Jack and Albert, 1920s. Photo: UPI/Corbis-Bettmann.*

Opposite, top left: *Russian-born Louis B. Mayer, head of production at MGM, c. 1935.*

Opposite, top right: *Samuel Goldwyn, who founded the Metro-Goldwyn-Mayer Company in 1925.*

Opposite, below: *Samuel Goldwyn with Jack Warner and his wife.*

A CLOSER LOOK:
JEWISH COMICS

It is hard to imagine 20th-century American comedy without the contribution of Jewish "funny people." *Time* magazine in 1978 claimed that although Jews made up only 3 percent of the American population, they made up a staggering 80 percent of its professional comedians. Their names run from "A"—Joey Adams, Woody Allen (nee Stewart Konigsberg), Morey Amsterdam—to "Z," namely Zero Mostel.

Even Jewish novelists, serious highbrow writers like Philip Roth, Saul Bellow, Joseph Heller, Norman Mailer, and Bernard Malamud laced their fiction of alienation and angst with uproarious humor. Their novels resonate with a kind of nervousness and witty social observation that makes readers laugh while they explore the hopelessness and absurdity of modern American life.

Scholars have tried to explain the connection between Jews and comedy. Some have seen it as a European holdover, a reaction of the oppressed to the enormity of their oppression. Such analysts have argued that humor served a therapeutic function. This answer is problematic in that it was in America where Jewish comedy blossomed most luxuriantly, and it is America where anti-Semitism has cropped up the least. Therefore, others who have tried to answer the question of why there are so many Jewish comics have looked to the Jewish tradition itself, particularly the long history of storytelling. Jews for centuries have celebrated the mid-winter holiday of Purim with parodies, skits, joking, and self-mockery.

So, too, perhaps the fact that Jews were marginal to America for generations helps to explain why they dominated American comedy. They were outsiders looking in, and they used comedy to parody the society they were learning to live in. They were also outsiders to traditional Jewish culture. They were American-born, or at least, American-raised, and the details of Jewish life in eastern Europe were the province of their parents and grandparents. They used comedy—intermixed with Yiddish words and idioms—to parody that world as well.

Whatever the explanation, from the late nineteenth century and the rise of vaudeville to the world of silent films and then talkies, from the Borscht Belt resorts to the television comedy hours and the stand-up comedy clubs, Jews helped Americans laugh.

Below, left: *Movie still of comedienne and Ziegfeld Follies' regular Fanny Brice. Photo: Corbis-Bettmann.*

Below, right: *"Last of the Red Hot Mommas" Sophie Tucker shows sailors aboard the U.S. Navy command ship* Adirondack *in 1952 how she got her reputation years earlier. Photo: UPI/Corbis-Bettmann.*

Andy Warhol. Ten Portraits of Jews of the 20th Century. The Marx Brothers. *1980. One from a portfolio of ten screenprints and colophon. 40 x 32 in. The Andy Warhol Foundation, Inc./Art Resource, New York. © 2001 Andy Warhol Foundation for the Visual Arts/ARS, New York.*

The Lower East Side, New York City, 1933.

Not surprisingly, many Jews, some of whose parents had come to America already influenced by socialist ideals, turned to left-wing politics to try to solve the nation's ills. A small number of Jews made up the majority of members of the Communist Party and other left-wing organizations.

Most Jews, however, even if they declared themselves to be socialists, enthusiastically embraced Franklin D. Roosevelt and his New Deal. More Jews served in the Roosevelt administration than had served in any previous administration: Sidney Hillman of the Amalgamated Clothing Workers' Union, Henry Morgenthau Jr., and Felix Frankfurter were among the most notable. In lower echelons of government, hundreds of young Jewish women and men went to work in the new programs in Washington, D.C.,, which they believed would bring prosperity, relieve suffering, and reform the economy.

To American Jews, Roosevelt's New Deal represented America's best chance. In it they saw the possibility of the United States government acting toward its citizens as the *kehilloth*, the Jewish communities, had toward

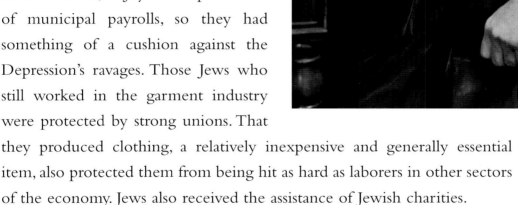

the Jews: providing a floor below which no one could fall and working on the principle that assistance toward those with need was not a matter of charity but the communal obligation of all.

Ironically, Jews as a group were somewhat less pinched by the economic downturn than many other Americans. Many of them either were self-employed or, as teachers and government workers, enjoyed the protection of municipal payrolls, so they had something of a cushion against the Depression's ravages. Those Jews who still worked in the garment industry were protected by strong unions. That they produced clothing, a relatively inexpensive and generally essential item, also protected them from being hit as hard as laborers in other sectors of the economy. Jews also received the assistance of Jewish charities.

Supreme Court Justice Felix Frankfurter. Franklin Roosevelt nominated Frankfurter to the Court in 1939. His earlier activities included teaching at Harvard Law, serving as chairman of the War Labor Policies Board during World War I, helping found the ACLU, and acting as legal advisor to the NAACP.

Other Americans may have noted this discrepancy, for while the 1910s and 1920s had witnessed the first emergence of significant anti-Semitism in America, it reached its high point in the 1930s. Americans facing unemployment and the loss of economic status behaved, at least on the surface, as many Christians had for centuries, blaming the Jews for their problems.

Of those Americans who disliked Roosevelt and his policies, some noted repeatedly that Roosevelt was surrounded by Jews. They questioned what they saw as the inordinate influence the Jews had upon Franklin Roosevelt and his activist wife, Eleanor, whom they frequently reviled as a "Jew-lover." Some referred to his administration as the "Jew Deal," and went so far as to claim that FDR was really a Jew named "Roosenfeld."

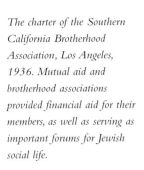

The charter of the Southern California Brotherhood Association, Los Angeles, 1936. Mutual aid and brotherhood associations provided financial aid for their members, as well as serving as important forums for Jewish social life.

American anti-Semites in the 1930s had a powerful model to follow. After all, this was the same decade in which Hitler assumed power in Germany, put into effect the Nuremberg Laws, and began the persecution of the Jews. Nazism even came to America. Agents from Germany helped organize the German American Bund, an organization intended to stir up pro-German sentiment in the United States and help convince Americans that the Jews were the enemies of the United States.

Despite all this, anti-Semitism was obviously more benign in America than in Germany, Poland, England, or France. But it was still frightening. Father Charles Coughlin of Detroit ranted over the radio to about thirty million listeners across the country about the Jewish domination of America. He appealed to readers of his newspaper *Social Justice*, which carried the same message. Gangs of teenagers in neighborhoods such as Yorkville in New York City desecrated synagogues and broke windows of Jewish stores.

In a number of urban African American neighborhoods, anti-Semitic rhetoric could be heard from street-corner speakers who blamed the Jews for the economic woes of the Black community. Many of the small merchants in Harlem, for example, were Jews, some of whom had been there since the days when mostly Jews lived on those streets. These merchants became the target of economic resentment, which then spilled over into a stream of anti-Jewish venom. On a more organized level, a campaign in Harlem to boycott merchants who did not hire African American employees, using the slogan "Don't Shop Where You Can't Work," targeted many small Jewish mom-and-pop stores.

These stores had long relied on the labor of family members. Particularly during the Depression, those who were able to hold onto their stores tried to help out unemployed relatives first. But in the eyes of Sufi El Hamid, the organizer of the campaign in Harlem, this made the Jews evil exploiters of Black people, and he claimed that he could easily sympathize with Hitler.

The kinds of job discrimination Jews had faced in the 1920s did not abate. Indeed, it was exacerbated in the face of the job shortages associated with the Depression. Jews with degrees in, for example, engineering found themselves selling tokens in the subway. They could not quantify how much of their difficulty in securing a position in their chosen field grew out of anti-Semitism and how much resulted from the Depression. When they saw others, non-Jews, get those jobs, however, many viewed anti-Semitism as the source of their problem.

Much American anti-Semitism existed exclusively on the level of rhetoric and tended to be associated with the bitterness of Americans caught in the Depression's tangled net. Some of it also reflected a belief that Jews represented city life and modernity, forces undermining small-town American values. But whatever the cause, it had powerful results. Most significant was that as the reality of the threat to Europe's Jews became apparent, Congress and the president refused to help.

All the efforts by American Jews to get Congress and the White House to intervene on behalf of refugees fell on deaf ears. Congress was heavily dominated by southerners, many of whom represented areas steeped in Christian fundamentalist thinking. Such areas were particularly wary, if not downright hostile, to Jews. Roosevelt depended on these congressmen and the voters behind them for his support. He could not appear overly solicitous of Jewish groups.

Most Jewish organizations recognized the reality of power politics in Washington, and they saw that the general mood in America did not favor easing the immigration restrictions for Jews. This pushed them toward adopting a quiet, behind-the-scenes approach when asking for consideration of their concerns. They staged no noisy rallies, no provocative demonstrations, believing that drawing attention to their Jewish agenda would only worsen anti-Semitism in America. History cannot be rewritten. But it is eerie to imagine what might have happened if the United States, recognizing the vast human tragedy unfolding in Europe, had welcomed Jews from Poland, Rumania, Germany, Hungary, and other places in Europe before they were caught by the invading German armies.

That did not happen, though, and much of American Jewish life in the 1930s was framed by a common awareness that outside their own neighborhoods and institutions, a relatively uncomfortable world existed.

What were Jews to do in the face of growing anti-Semitism in America? On a communal level, Jews shied away from drawing attention to their own concerns, and they sought instead to build alliances with other Americans. They tended to combat anti-Semitism at a general level, by attacking all forms of prejudice. When they sought legislation to bar discrimination, they highlighted the ways in which all Americans were hurt by practices that singled out people by race, religion, or national origin.

The real prejudice against Jews hurt young people the most. Many thought that the obstacles to "making it" as Jews were insurmountable. As a result, many changed their names, so that when they applied for jobs, no one

would guess they were Jews. Many others just turned away from Jewish community life and Judaism because it brought them pain, humiliation, and needless hardship rather than a sense of well-being and solidarity.

For rabbis and Jewish educators, this alienation of young American Jews from Judaism was actually a much greater problem than all the scurrilous anti-Semitic newspaper articles and speeches. First, it had become clear that European Jewry was being destroyed and that America would become the center of Jewish life. Second, since a majority of the Jewish population in America was made up of American-born children of immigrants, the future of American Jewry lay in their hands. Thus, young American Jews had to find a way to embrace Judaism at the same time as they were struggling to be accepted as Americans.

The dilemma of this generation of American Jews was captured most powerfully in a book, *Judaism as a Civilization,* published in 1934 by Rabbi

Socialist parade.). For many American Jews, their socialist politics came as a natural extension of their support of trade unionism. The strong Jewish attraction to socialism first developed in eastern Europe, and it was imported to America by both Jewish men and women.

"Learn to Vote" campaign, 1938.

Mordecai Kaplan. Kaplan himself had been born in eastern Europe. He came to America as a young child, and was one of the early graduates of the Jewish Theological Seminary.

He began his rabbinical career as an Orthodox rabbi but increasingly found himself unable to reconcile traditional Judaism with American ideals. In *Judaism as a Civilization*, in the synagogue he created (the Society for the Advancement of Judaism), and in his long career teaching at the Jewish Theological Seminary, he spoke about the crisis he had endured, which he believed was the crisis of most educated American Jews.

Kaplan argued that American Jews lived in two civilizations, Jewish and American. The two worlds had to harmonize with each other in order for

Judaism to maintain the loyalty of its American daughters and sons, and it was Judaism that had to accommodate itself to America. American Jews had the right to tinker with tradition to make it fit American democratic values. They had to find ways to alter Jewish rituals and principles so that they were consistent with America and, at the same time, served a Jewish purpose. He coined the aphorism that "*halacha* [Jewish law] should have a vote, but not a veto" as American Jews created new forms and texts for worship.

He noted, for example, that in America, women had achieved a measure of equality. But in Judaism they sat in the back of the synagogue silently with no public role. His daughter Judith became the first girl in the millennia-old history of the Jewish tradition to be called to the Torah at age thirteen to mark her bat mitzvah. Until that day only boys, who became bar mitzvah, could be honored with achieving adulthood this way.

Theresa Bernstein. Zionist Meeting, New York. *1923. Oil on canvas. 34 1/2 x 44 1/2 in. Jewish National Fund.*

But Kaplan saw the problem as more than changing the liturgy or adding new ceremonies. He believed that Jewish life had to be based around an organic community life. After all, communities were what held people together, and Jews in America would not be committed to Judaism unless it helped them achieve a good and comfortable life. He envisioned "synagogue-centers," where Jews could worship, meet with friends, enjoy the arts, even participate in athletics, all under the roof of a single Jewish institution.

In the 1930s, his ideas, as expressed in *Judaism as a Civilization,* led to the formation of the Reconstructionist movement, the fourth and smallest denomination within the construct of American Judaism. It was not until the late 1960s that the Reconstructionists actually established a seminary to train their own rabbis. Thus, from the 1930s onward, their numbers were drawn from the graduates of the Conservative movement's seminary, the Jewish Theological Seminary, and from that of its Reform equivalent, the Hebrew Union College.

Kaplan was also a Zionist. He believed that the budding Jewish society that was being constructed in Palestine by the women and men of the *yishuv* represented the best way for American Jews to see Judaism as a creative force. He believed that Zionist activity in America, particularly in the form

One of the most famous (and notorious) institutions of American Jewish life was the afternoon school. The modern equivalent of the traditional heder, *it was attended by both Jewish boys and girls after the public school day ended. Educators, worried that Jewish children disliked attending, sought new ways and new materials to make the experience "fun."*

of summer camps for youngsters, could provide a meaningful and dynamic focus for Jewish identity.

Zionists had been active in America from the end of the nineteenth century, when the movement developed in Europe as well. But the Zionist organizations never enlisted the support or membership of very many American Jews. Hadassah, the women's Zionist organization, was a powerful exception. Through the remarkable leadership of Henrietta Szold, who oversaw the organization's work raising money for health and welfare projects in Palestine, Hadassah had by the 1920s become the largest Jewish organization in America.

Rita Judashko, age 4. Washington Heights, New York, 1942. Washington Heights was famous for its community of German Jewish refugees, many of whom arrived during the 1930s.

But as a rule, Zionism as a political ideology was not a major force in American Jewish life. Most of the Jews who had come from eastern Europe—with the exception of some on the left—supported the idea of a Jewish homeland, but relatively few belonged to any Zionist organization.

The Reform movement had opposed the idea of creating a Jewish homeland in Palestine. Throughout the early twentieth century, Reform leaders articulated the idea that America was their home, and they did not want their non-Jewish fellow citizens to think that they wanted a different home. Still, individual Reform rabbis and laypeople took a different approach. Stephen Wise, Abba Hillel Silver, and James Heller, all Reform rabbis, and Julian Mack, a layman affiliated with Reform, were in the 1920s, 1930s, and 1940s among the most prominent leaders of American Zionism.

The gathering clouds in Germany, however, changed much about the way Jews in America related to the Zionist ideal. What had seemed just a romantic and impractical dream appeared by the middle of the 1930s to be possibly the only solution to the emerging tragedy. In 1938, after the passage of the Nuremberg Laws in Germany, which stripped Jews of their citizenship, the German annexation of Austria, which brought tens of

A CLOSER LOOK:
ALBERT EINSTEIN

Considered by many the greatest scientific thinker of the twentieth century, German-born Albert Einstein came to America in 1933 under the looming shadow of the Third Reich. He had done much of his paradigm-shattering scientific work in Germany, receiving the Nobel prize for physics in 1921 for his explanation of the photoelectric effect. The prize and his articles on relativity and Brownian movement won him a professorship at the University of Zurich in Switzerland. In 1916 he moved to an even more prestigious position at the Prussian Academy of Science in Berlin. In the late 1910s and 1920s the public at large became aware of Einstein, and his name became synonymous with the idea of scientific genius.

In 1933, however, Hitler had come to power in Germany, and Einstein, sensing the danger, resigned his position in Berlin and accepted an offer of a professorship at the Institute for Advanced Study in Princeton. Einstein vowed that he would never return to Germany, and he became an American citizen.

During World War II he, in conjunction with a number of other scientists, many of them also Jewish refugees from Nazi Germany, helped developed the atomic weaponry program of the United States. Einstein and his colleague Leo Szilard, another refugee, were involved in developing the Manhattan Project. But Einstein opposed the idea of developing an atomic bomb. He participated in the founding of the Emergency Committee of Atomic Scientists, which urged the outlawing of nuclear weapons.

Einstein was also an active member of the worldwide Jewish community. He helped raise money for Jewish causes and lectured widely on the plight of the Jews of Germany and the need for a Jewish homeland in Palestine. He was actually approached by Israel's first prime minister, David Ben-Gurion, with the proposition that he become president of Israel, an offer Einstein refused.

Below: Albert Einstein beside a blackboard, 1921.
Background: Albert Einstein holding an informal seminar at the Institute of Advanced Learning, c. 1940s/1950s.
Photo: Corbis-Bettman.

Albert Einstein at a dinner in his honor by the American Palestine campaign committee, late 1920s, with Felix M. Warburg (seated left), Mrs. Einstein (seated right), (standing left to right: Robert Szold, president of the Zionist Organization of America, Morris Rothenberg, chairman of American Palestine Campaign, Rabbi Stephen Wise, Jefferson Seligman. Photo © Corbis-Bettman.

A CLOSER LOOK:
HENRIETTA SZOLD

Henrietta Szold, a native of Baltimore, founded in 1912 the world's largest Jewish organization to date, Hadassah. Originally named Daughters of Zion, Hadassah was an association for women that focused on the health needs of the people of Palestine, both Arabs and Jews. In Palestine Hadassah was responsible for building Hadassah Hospital, arguably the finest medical facility in the Middle East and one of the leading medical institutions in the world

In the United States Hadassah was a powerful organizing force in the lives of middle-class Jewish women. It offered a focus for their political, cultural, social, and charitable efforts.

Szold also played a role in the intellectual life of American Jewry. She translated dozens of Hebrew works into English and prepared them for publication. For a number of years she edited the *American Jewish Yearbook*, and helped compile the *Jewish Encyclopedia*. Szold was likewise a powerful force in American Zionism, both before and after her creation of Hadassah. She pursued for herself and her organization an independent identity within the ranks of the Zionist movement and did not yield to pressure from her male colleagues.

Szold also played a dramatic role in the unfolding tragedy of the Jews of Germany. In the 1930s she became director of Youth

Aliyah, an effort to bring German Jewish young people out of the perils of Germany to Palestine. She was in Palestine in 1934 to greet the first group of teenagers who were rescued from almost certain death in Germany. At the end of World War II, millions of Jewish children were left orphaned, and Szold worked tirelessly to get immigration certificates for thirty thousand of them to come to Palestine, despite the opposition of the British government.

Above: *Henrietta Szold. Photo: UPI/Corbis-Bettmann.*

Below: *The first graduating class of nurses from Hadassah Hospital, 1922. Henrietta Szold, the founder of Hadassah, is seated in the center of the photo.*

thousands of Jews under Hitler's control, and the German occupation of Czechoslovakia, which imperiled another large Jewish community, the rabbis of the Reform movement met in Columbus, Ohio, and issued a statement of principles that was essentially a rewriting of the text originally issued in 1885 in Pittsburgh.

The Reform movement reflected the broad base of American Jewish public opinion. Thus, the 1940s, during and after World War II, were a high point for membership in Zionist societies. American Jews raised money, from nickels and dimes collected on street corners to more substantial contributions from those who could afford it, to help the Zionist effort. And, when World War II ended and the extent of the carnage became evident, individual American Jews and their congregations and organizations cheered on the efforts by the Jews in Palestine to force the British out and declare a Jewish state, the state of Israel.

Baseball player Hank Greenberg of the Detroit Tigers swings his bat at home plate during a game, 1938. Hank Greenberg's finest baseball moment was in September 1934, when Hank refused to play on Yom Kippur. His team was in hot pursuit of the American League pennant. Despite the pressure on him to play and the anti-Semitism that was at its height during the Depression, Greenberg put down his bat and mitt, put on his prayershawl, and joined his fellow Jews at Yom Kippur services.

In the half century after 1948, that state in the Middle East shaped much about American Jewish political life. So, too, the memories of the slaughter in Europe haunted the Jews, including their children born in later decades.

Meanwhile, American Jews emerged from World War II a more affluent and middle-class group than they had been at its start. Hundreds of thousands of young Jewish men took advantage of the G.I. Bill and completed their college educations. Hundreds of thousands of young Jewish families took advantage of the boom in suburban housing and moved out to new communities, where they created Jewish life as they saw fit.

Military chaplaincy, at a service in the Marianas, 1944.

Still, however much Jews became prime beneficiaries of the prosperity of the post–World War II era, the events of the 1930s and 1940s—the virulent

175

anti-Semitism, the powerful bonds between themselves and Jews around the world—remained with them. By the end of World War II, America had emerged as the single largest Jewish community in the world. How would American Jews, who were now moving en masse to the suburban frontiers, handle that responsibility?

Celebrating Hanukkah. St. Paul, Minnesota, c. 1940.

Hebrew text on monument (right-to-left):

ווו בימך ארזרור
צורוף אשר בא או
תורה יב יצא
זה לפניך להכות
במסנה פלשתים

Ben Shahn

A GOLDEN AGE
(1948–1967)

I f any era could be considered a "golden age" in the history of American Jewry, the twenty years following World War II would come closest. In these years, American Jews put their troubled memories of the recent past—the pinch of the Depression, the anti-Semitism of the 1920s and 1930s, and the horrors of the war—on hold.

American Jews, of course, did not forget these relatively recent crises. Recollections of these traumas echoed in how they confronted the openness of the new era. In post–World War II America, however, they focused on the expansion of opportunities and the relative absence of barriers in a liberalized American climate.

One of the most notable characteristics of this period involved the trouncing of anti-Semitism. Changes occurred in neighborhoods and institutions of work, learning, and leisure that had once treated Jews differently from other Americans. Colleges and universities that in earlier eras had maintained quotas against Jews now dropped them or just failed to enforce these highly discriminatory practices any longer.

The Jewish community, as an organized body, had in the past seen discrimination in higher education as one of its greatest burdens. In fact, at the end of World War II, a number of Jewish academics and intellectuals decided that Jews faced so many burdens in the area of admission to higher education that it was time for them to create a Jewish-sponsored university.

Until that time the only undergraduate college with a Jewish affiliation was Yeshiva University, which had maintained bachelor's-level programs since the 1930s. But Orthodoxy represented only a small minority among American Jews, and the vast majority never would have considered attending Yeshiva, with its separate campuses for men and women and its emphasis on traditional practice.

Out of the post-World War II efforts, then, emerged Brandeis University in 1948, a nonsectarian university that functioned under Jewish auspices and offered a strong program in Judaic studies.

A Hillel Executive Council, 1951. Founded in 1923, Hillel continues to act as the major provider of Jewish services on American university campuses. Many American Jews credit Hillel as the critical influence on their Jewish self-awareness.

By the 1960s, 80 percent of young Jews entered higher education. Moreover, when they arrived on campuses, public and private, large and small, they found something that an earlier generation of Jewish college students had not found: Jewish faculty members.

In earlier periods, higher education had been one of the most discriminatory sectors of the American economy. It was very difficult for Jews to be hired and receive tenure in most universities, particularly in fields such as history, classics, and literature. By the 1950s, academia eased its barriers, and Jews increasingly pursued graduate degrees in all fields; by the end of the 1960s one-tenth of all professors were Jewish. The educational triumphs of the 1960s helped push aside the memories of past discrimination and poverty.

The castle, a major Brandeis University landmark, was recently featured on a U.S. postal card to celebrate the university's 50th year. The campus is located in Waltham, a Boston suburb.

Other areas of American life also opened up for Jews. In the field of housing, Jews began to move into neighborhoods once limited to gentiles. In 1948 the U.S. Supreme Court issued a ruling in the case *Shelly vs. Kramer* declaring that restricted covenants were unenforceable. In the past, under restricted covenants, people who bought houses might be asked to sign codicils to their deeds in which they promised that they would never sell to Jews or Black people.

Moreover, after 1945, many states began to pass civil rights legislation. New York did so first that year, and most northern states followed in the next decade and a half. In 1964 and 1965 Congress passed sweeping legislation that outlawed discrimination in public accommodations, employment, housing, and education, whether based on race, religion, national origin, or sex.

Jews were among the main and earliest beneficiaries of these legislative triumphs against unequal treatment. In New York, after its legislature enacted the civil rights bill, Jews sued employers who refused to hire them, resorts that refused to accommodate them, and real-estate agents who would not sell or rent to them.

Jews, as members of an organized community, were ever conscious of the fact that they had just come through one of the most horrendous eras in the history of their people. While they did not engage in extensive public discourse on the slaughter of European Jewry, the lingering images of that calamity pushed them into working for a world based on intergroup understanding.

With this hope in mind, American Jews worked actively on the national, state, and local levels with other civil rights organizations to promote civil rights bills, and in the process, they helped change the climate of American life. Through organizations such as the American Jewish Committee, the American Jewish Congress, the Anti-Defamation League, and on the local level, various Jewish Community Councils, Jews cooperated and often led the effort to change both the laws and public opinion. The message they wanted to give Americans was that prejudice was wrong, whether directed at African Americans, Jews, or anyone else. On a legislative level, they wanted to make it illegal.

Throughout this period Jews continued to vote solidly as liberals in all elections. They embraced the legacy of the New Deal and the expansion of the government's role in bringing about a more equitable society.

Significantly, these liberal politics of American Jews took place in the complicated atmosphere of the Cold War. Jews supported liberal causes and were advocates of free speech and free expression. At the same time, many who were anti-Communist crusaders tended to lump liberal causes—civil

rights, support for the United Nations, advocacy of civil liberties—with Communism. Furthermore, many of the most rabid anti-Communists also tended to spout the kind of anti-Semitic rhetoric that had been so common in the 1920s. They associated Jews with international Communism and accused American Jews of being "fellow travelers" or closet sympathizers with the Soviet Union.

These anti-Communists who considered all Jews to be potential agents of Communism had powerful ammunition in their arsenal, for in the summer of 1950, a Jewish couple, Ethel and Julius Rosenberg, were arrested on charges of passing atomic secrets to the Soviet Union. One of their friends, Morton Sobel, also Jewish, was arrested as well. Ethel Rosenberg's brother, David Greenglass, and his wife, Ruth, were also taken into custody. Ethel and Julius Rosenberg were tried, found guilty, and in 1953 went to the electric chair at Sing Sing Prison for their betrayal of the United States.

Martin Luther King, Jr., and Rabbi Abraham Heschel were among the leaders of the silent vigil for peace staged in February 1968 at the base of the Tomb of the Unknowns in Arlington Cemetery in protest against the war in Vietnam.

Julius and Ethel Rosenberg, wearing handcuffs, kiss in the back of a prison van after their treason arraignment, New York City. The Rosenbergs were the only people executed as Soviet spies during the Cold War. To this day, people question the severity of their punishment. Subsequent research has pointed to Julius's guilt and Ethel's innocence.

A great deal of historical detection work has gone on in the decades since the execution of the Rosenbergs to determine if either or both of them was actually guilty, and if so, whether their actions made a real difference in the struggle between the Soviet Union and the United States. Regardless of the answer, their arrest, trial, and execution had a tremendous impact on American Jews, who had just decades before been labeled as unassimilable, and who for centuries had been scapegoats for the anxieties and fears of others. Now, the fact that at the height of American anti-Communism, the two people executed by the United States government for their political actions happened to be Jewish sent a shudder of fear down the spine of American Jews.

Indeed, most Jews had moved away from the left-wing culture that had flourished in the immigrant neighborhoods. The immigrant generation was dwindling in numbers, and their socialist politics and cultural institutions did not particularly appeal to their children and grandchildren. Much of the socialist fervor had been generated through the Jewish unions and other workers' organizations. But the Jews of the 1950s and 1960s were professionals and businesspeople, not furriers, milliners, and garment workers.

In fact, Jews were becoming leaders in nearly every area of American life. And to every endeavor they brought a deep reverence for their culture and history, from business, politics, and law to literature, art, music, and theater. With increasing success, Jewish Americans were living the American dream, while never losing sight of their Jewishness.

A CLOSER LOOK:
JONAS SALK AND ALBERT SABIN

The fight against polio was waged and won by two Jewish scientists. First, Jonas Salk, a physician and microbiologist, born in New York City in 1914, developed a polio vaccine in the mid-1950s. Like many Jewish New Yorkers, he graduated from the City College of New York. Then he went on to get a medical degree at New York University in 1939. In the 1940s, as a faculty member at the University of Michigan, he began to study the disease that was ravaging America. Even the president of the United States, Franklin Roosevelt, had been its victim.

Salk did much of his research at the University of Pittsburgh, where he developed the vaccine that was made by cultivating three strains of the virus in monkey tissue. He separated the tissue, stored it, and then killed it with formaldehyde. The Salk vaccine, which children around America in the 1950s lined up to get, required a series of three or four injections.

Another front in the war on polio was launched by Albert Sabin. Sabin was an immigrant. He had come to the United States in 1921, when he was fifteen, from Bialystok, Poland. He received his medical training at New York University, and between 1942 and 1953 he worked on the problem of polio. In the mid-1950s he developed a polio strain that was live and was administered orally.

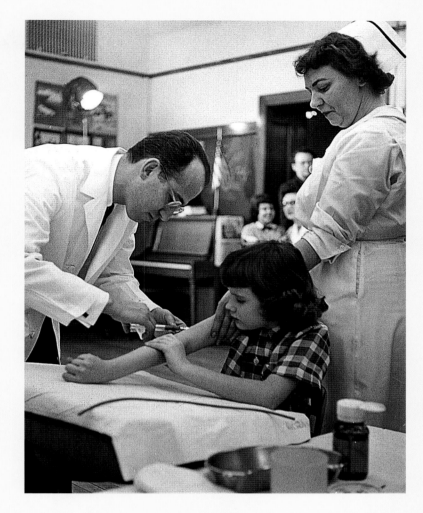

While scientists have debated the merits of the two forms of the vaccine, there is no question that the scientists who discovered them radically eliminated the scourge of the crippling disease.

In 1962, Salk established the Salk Institute for Biological Studies, in La Jolla, California. He did research on multiple sclerosis and cancer and devoted the last years of his life to working on HIV research. In 1977, Dr. Jonas Salk received the nation's highest civilian honor—the Presidential Medal of Freedom.

The Sabin oral vaccine became available in 1960. Today, Albert Sabin's oral vaccine for polio is the form most widely used throughout the world. Although best known for his research into polio, Sabin also researched and developed vaccines for a number of other infectious diseases.

Above: *Dr. Jonas Salk administering an injection of polio vaccine.*

Left: *Dr. Albert Sabin with his records containing thirty years of polio research.*
Photo: © Bettmann/CORBIS.

Above, left: *Born in Canada in 1915, Saul Bellow is one of the great American and Jewish voices of modern literature. He won the Nobel Prize for Literature in 1976.*

Above, right: *Although a Yiddish writer, Isaac Bashevis Singer has long been more popular with English audiences. He arrived in the U.S. from Poland in 1935, following his equally talented brother, I. J. Singer. He also won the Nobel Prize for Literature, in 1978.*

Many notable faces of the twentieth century are Jewish. Jews became important figures in the American literary scene: Philip Roth, Saul Bellow, and Bernard Malamud. Leonard Bernstein, the first *American*-born conductor of the New York Philharmonic, brought classical music not only to new heights, but also onto television screens and into millions of American homes. Sandy Koufax, like Hank Greenberg in the 1930s, was a popular baseball star, and like his predecessor, he refused to play on Yom Kippur. In 1947 the country even had a Jewish Miss America, Bess Meyerson.

While Senda Berenson was teaching at Smith College, she learned about a new game, "basket ball." She introduced the game to the women's college, and wrote the official rule book for women's collegiate basketball. In 1984, thirty years after her death, Senda Berenson was the first woman inducted into the Basketball Hall of Fame in Springfield, Massachusetts.

Out of the spotlight of celebrity, however, the story of American Jewish daily life in post–World War II America took place in the suburbs. Most of these towns, which lay just beyond the city limits, were new communities. Built by developers, many of whom in New York and New Jersey were Jewish, and buttressed by federal housing and highway policy, these suburbs

were havens for young white families. Black families had little chance to participate in this exodus, as they were too poor, and discriminatory practices kept them out.

Typically, young men returned from military service, married, and moved to these communities, where housing was inexpensive, but roomy. They settled among others like themselves, young couples with new babies in tow. They created a style of life and a cultural milieu built around family life, recreation for couples, and the educational and social needs of their growing children.

Jews flocked to predominantly Jewish suburbs, just as Italian Americans went to particular communities and Irish Americans to others. But these suburban communities generally tended to be less homogeneous than the urban neighborhoods the young couples were leaving.

Sandy Koufax in his Los Angeles Dodgers uniform, 1965. Sandy Koufax and Hank Greenberg share the distinction of being the only Jewish members of the Baseball Hall of Fame, and they share the distinction of opting for Judaism over baseball at a crucial moment. Koufax was pitching for his team during the 1965 World Series, but when one of the games conflicted with Yom Kippur he knew what to do, and like Greenberg, did not play.

In the new suburban communities Jews and non-Jews lived in general harmony with each other. They joined together in PTAs to ensure the quality of their children's public schools. They had a common interest in maintaining public libraries, playgrounds, and shopping facilities. In the process, little religious or ethnic hostility surfaced.

The city neighborhoods where Jews had lived, and which couples with children were leaving, had been characterized by an unmistakable Jewish flavor and texture. Neighborhoods in the Bronx, for example, had kosher butcher shops, kosher bakeries, other food shops that catered to Jewish tastes, Yiddish schools, Hebrew schools, and the storefront offices of Jewish

A CLOSER LOOK:
LEONARD BERNSTEIN

The first American-born conductor to lead the New York Philharmonic, Leonard Bernstein was born in 1918 in Lawrence, Massachusetts. Bernstein took upon himself the cause of making classical music accessible to American young people. For fifteen years he hosted a televised series, *Young People's Concerts*, intended to expose young and old alike to classical music. Thus, he helped to take this genre of music out of the exclusive domain of elite culture.

Bernstein also was a serious composer. He sometimes turned to Jewish sources for inspiration, writing such symphonic works as *Chichester Psalms* (in Hebrew), *Jeremiah*, and *Kaddish*. Bernstein also composed for the theater. His scores for *On the Town*, *Candide*, and particularly *West Side Story*—an adaptation of Shakespeare's *Romeo and Juliet* set in a tough urban neighborhood—achieved worldwide renown for the composer and American musical culture.

Bernstein maintained extremely close ties to Israel. In 1948, while the Israeli war for independence was raging, Bernstein conducted the Israel Philharmonic. In 1967 he flew to Israel upon the conclusion of the Six-Day War and conducted a victory concert with such gestures and involvement, he helped build the infrastructure of a music culture in Israel.

Above: *Bernstein playing piano for a group of children, New York City, 1958.*

Below: *Bernstein in performance, c. 1968.*

Opposite: *Bernstein showing the components of a symphony on television's "Omnibus."*

Gregory Peck starred as Phil Green in Gentleman's Agreement *(1947), directed by Elia Kazan. The film was a remarkably uncompromising look at the issue of anti-Semitism in the workplace of the 1940s.*

organizations, all visible on the street. Newspaper stands sold Yiddish newspapers. Since the older generation did not join the move to the suburbs, however, neither did the full range of Jewish institutions. As a consequence, the kinds of public spaces that developed in the suburbs downplayed ethnic distinctiveness.

Suburban Jewish life revolved around synagogues, and from the end of World War II through the early 1960s there was an explosion in synagogue construction. In some cases, older, urban congregations were transplanted to the suburbs, following the population out of the cities. In other cases, new congregations were formed by the residents of new communities.

A greater percentage of Jews belonged to synagogues in these years than at any time before (with the exception of the eighteenth century) or since. Synagogues provided places for Jewish parents to send their children for Jewish education, particularly bar mitzvah instruction for the boys. Synagogues were also the places to mark life cycle events and for Jews to enjoy leisure-time activities with other Jews. Classes and clubs met in the synagogues: men's clubs, sisterhoods, teen groups, theatrical groups, Scout troops, nursery schools. Synagogues had gift shops where families could buy ritual objects, many of which were imported from Israel, a country whose

A CLOSER LOOK:
ROCK & ROLL

In 1951, Leo Mintz, the owner of a record store in Cleveland, convinced Alan Freed, a radio show host at WXEL, to host a new show, one which featured rhythm and blues music. Freed agreed and under the pseudonym of Moondog, he took to the air. With that name he changed American music and the English language. His show was called "Moondog's Rock and Roll Party." With these words and this music a revolution in America was born.

With its fusion of African-American music, played to racially integrated audiences and featured at concerts and dance parties across the country, America's racial hierarchy was threatened and its youth culture launched.

Freed, who himself had played with a band called Sultans of Swing, was part of a cadre of American Jews who made rock and roll possible. Others in this cadre were the brothers Phil and Leonard Chess, who came from Poland in the late 1920s, and operated a nightclub in Chicago on the city's predominantly black South Side. The Chess brothers started recording the artists who performed there, first on their Aristocrat label, and then on the even more significant "Chess Records," which brought such musicians as

Muddy Waters, Chuck Berry, Bo Diddly, and Howlin' Wolf into the homes of many Americans. Indeed in 1951, the year Moondog—Alan Freed—took to the air with his rock and roll show, the Chess brothers recorded Jackie Brenson's album, "Rocket 88," deemed by many the very first rock and roll record.

In 1945 Syd Nathan launched his King Records in Cincinnati. His was the first company to market white and black artists on the same label. It was Syd Nathan who recorded James Brown, an icon of American rock and roll.

Nathan, the Chess Brothers, and Alan Freed, along with Jerry Leiber and Mike Stoller—songwriters who wrote for "Big Mama" Thornton and Ben E. King—all stood behind the scenes as rock and roll took off. As owners of record companies, managers, promoters, and songwriters, they helped create a distinctive style that brought young people from both sides of America's racial divide into a common culture.

American rock music disc jockey Alan Freed with two female fans.

A CLOSER LOOK:
MUSIC, DANCE, AND THEATER

The impact of Jewish Americans on our performing arts is astounding. The immigrants to the United States from Europe included some of the most talented artists in music, dance, art, and drama. They brought this gift with them and gave generously to generations of Americans.

Left: Actor and comedian Zero Mostel during the original Broadway production of A Funny Thing Happened on the Way to the Forum, *c. 1962. Mostel also starred in the film version.*

Below: Richard Rodgers and Oscar Hammerstein, 1960. The team brought to American musical theater a more realistic form, with fully developed stories and characters as well as songs that were woven into the plot.

Opposite, top left: Legendary choreographer Jerome Robbins changed our idea of dance in both the classical dance world and musical theater, giving it a distinctly American flavor. Photo: © Bettmann/CORBIS.

Opposite, top right: Popular Boston Pops conductor Arthur Fiedler, 1961.

Opposite, bottom: Artur Rubinstein, 1958. Rubinstein made his professional debut as a pianist at the age of 11. Trained in Berlin, he was best known for his performances of late-19th-century Romantic composers. Photo: Corbis-Bettmann.

A CLOSER LOOK:
FILM

By the middle of the 20th century, there were a host of Jewish screenwriters, directors, producers, and actors behind the scenes, behind the camera, and in front of the camera. The 1960s saw the emergence of an increasing ethnic awareness on the silver screen. Jewish actors began to play Jewish roles, and Jewish subjects were often approached in powerful terms. Both dramas and comedies alike tackled important historical events and complicated social issues, from the horrors of the Holocaust in movies such as *Judgment at Nuremberg* (1961) to the establishment of the state of Israel in *Exodus* (1960), to Sholem Aleichem's stories of life in a Russian *shtetl* in *Fiddler on the Roof* (1969).

Left: *Paul Newman as the hero, Ari Ben-Canaan, in the film version of Leon Uris's book,* Exodus, *about the founding of the state of Israel. The film was directed by Otto Preminger.*

Below: Exodus *director Otto Preminger enjoys a hearty, behind-the-scenes laugh.*

Opposite, top: *Dramatist, actor, and director Clifford Odets, probably during the filming of* None But the Lonely Heart.

Opposite, bottom: *Director Stanley Kubrick at work.*

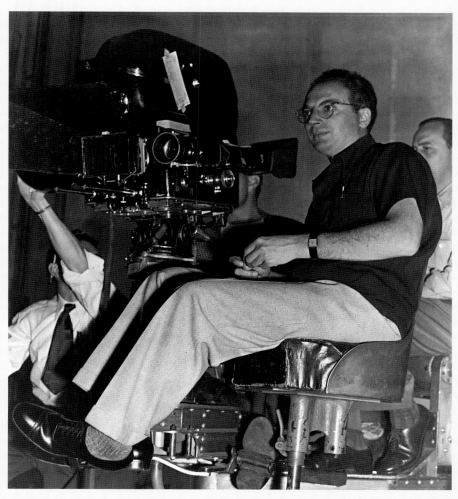

Chickens hanging in a kosher poultry store. Photo: © Bettmann/CORBIS.

struggles and achievements elicited the sympathy of American Jews.

Only a few Orthodox synagogues made the move to the suburbs during these years. Most Orthodox Jews tended to be poorer and older than the rest of the American Jewish population, and they stayed put in their city neighborhoods. The Conservative movement, dedicated as it was to both being modern and retaining much of traditional practice, had the most difficult time with the demands of life in suburbia.

Ironically, the Conservative movement was the major beneficiary of the suburbanization of the 1950s and 1960s, emerging in these years as the single largest American Jewish denomination.

The suburban synagogues, Reform or Conservative, came to be heavily dominated by the activism and energy of women. Jewish women, like other middle-class suburbanites, tended to drop out of the labor market when they had young children, especially if their husbands earned comfortable incomes. Many of the women were highly educated, and a large number had been teachers, social workers, and librarians before their children were born. Often, they went back to these professions when their children entered school.

But in the years that they chose not to be employed, they enriched much of suburban synagogue life. These women constituted the core and back-

bone of the voluntary sector of the congregations. They ran the libraries and gift shops. They directed the education committees and many, as unpaid teachers, taught the children. They also oversaw the social events that drew members to the building.

Outside the synagogues, suburban Jewish women who did not have to earn an income also created a vast range of Jewish voluntary associations. Some labored for the federations, the local Jewish fund-raising bodies that collected money for international, national, and local Jewish needs. Others joined the National Council of Jewish Women, Hadassah, ORT, or the Brandeis Women's Clubs, some of the more popular Jewish women's organizations that sustained Jewish community life along with the sisterhoods of the synagogues.

In the face of their enormous contribution to the Jewish communities, women began to assume roles in the synagogue services. Until the 1950s

Rutgers University students dancing the horah at a campus social. University campuses were an important site for growing interest in Jewish culture and Judaism. This interest was part of the counterculture movement of the 1960s.

women sat through services as observers. The Conservative movement in the 1950s decided that women could be called to the Torah to recite the blessings. In Reform and Conservative congregations, girls started celebrating their bat mitzvah, though not in the same way as their brothers marked their bar mitzvah. But at least a space for women in the public performance of Judaism was emerging. Change in the status of women was in the air.

Other changes could be observed. In the aftermath of World War II small communities of Orthodox Jews, survivors of the Holocaust, settled in America. In neighborhoods like Brooklyn's Williamsburg, Crown Heights, and Boro Park, as well as in Lakewood, New Jersey, and Monsey, in Rockland County, New York, they tried to do something that had never been done in America before: establish all-Jewish *Hasidic* communities made up of women and men who had no interest in "fitting in." They had no doubt that they wanted to remain separate from American culture, that living lives based on traditional Judaism was vastly superior to achieving American success and acceptance.

In summary, in the post–World War II "golden age," the Jewish American embrace of Israel and the memorialization of the Holocaust were powerful themes. But they paled in comparison to what would follow. The year 1967 was a watershed in American Jewish life, and the developments of the postwar era set the stage for the shifts to take place in the decades to come.

Reading the Torah.

SEARCHING
FOR CONTINUITY
(1967–2000)

The last three decades of the twentieth century were surely an era of contrasts in the lives of American Jews. In the thirty-plus years from 1967 to 2000 two distinct paths emerged: one in which Jews were more committed to the Jewish component of their lives, and another that found Jews less involved with that part of their identity.

Judaism as a religion was firmly ensconced as one of America's core faith traditions. Observant Jewish men unselfconsciously wore *kippot*, skullcaps, on their heads wherever they went: baseball stadiums, prestigious law firms, university lecture halls. Jewish parents gave their children Hebrew names, both those of biblical derivation and those of modern Israeli origin. They no longer felt the need to hide their identities in public.

Furthermore, Jewish themes became the subject of much of American popular culture, and Yiddish words—*shlepp, hutzpah, kvetch*—entered into common American parlance. A revolution had taken place in the comfort level of American Jews in terms of how they presented themselves to non-Jews. The reticence with which they had once behaved both politically and culturally was dropped, and many felt comfortable proclaiming their distinctive identities and particularistic needs.

Opposite: *Synagogue morning service, 1991. The women's section (the balcony) indicates an Orthodox synagogue. Despite the traditional service and seating arrangements, the building's architectural style is quite modern, the consequence of acculturation, suburbanization, and affluence.*

Hasidic Jews reading bulletins, Brooklyn, New York, 1972. The major influx of Hasidic Jews to the U.S. came after the Holocaust. A long-term consequence of this immigration has been to encourage more rigorous observance of halacha (Jewish law) across the Orthodox world. Photo: © Nathan Benn / CORBIS.

As mentioned at the end of the last chapter, a small but growing handful of the ultra-orthodox, particularly through the Habad movement of the Lubavitch *Hasidim*, began to play a more prominent role in American Jewish life. They lived primarily in their own communities, and they maintained their own synagogues and educational institutions, stores, and even in some cases, transportation systems.

In places such as Boro Park and Williamsburg in Brooklyn and Monsey in New York's Rockland County, *Hasidim* sects who lived together in solid units became forceful in local politics. Since their leader, their *rebbe*, could deliver all the votes of the group, American politicians, congressional representatives, city council members, mayors—and even governors and senators—visited them and tried to meet their demands. These Jews had little to do with the majority of American Jews, but their presence affected all.

In contrast, for a more and more American Jews, Jewishness had receded in importance. While they did not convert to Christianity nor actively or affir-

matively renounce their Jewishness, it ceased to define how they functioned.

From the late 1960s on, the levels of personal observance of Jewish ritual, as expressed through *kashrut*, any kind of Sabbath observance, Jewish education for children, synagogue membership, or membership in any Jewish organization, dropped precipitously. Jewish families also moved to communities and neighborhoods that did not have large clusterings of Jews or Jewish institutions. More Jewish children lived, went to school, and socialized mainly among non-Jews.

Rates of intermarriage soared. By the 1990s, in some communities, such as Denver, half of all young Jews were marrying non-Jews. Other communities had lower rates of intermarriage, but they still hovered around 30 percent. While some of the non-Jewish spouses converted to Judaism, most did not. Jewish educators, rabbis, and community leaders worried that over time intermarriage would sap American Jewry of numbers and of a sense of bonding to the "eternal people."

A young Jewish girl preparing for her bat mitzvah. In recent decades, American Jewish women have come to enjoy privileges previously available only to men, such as bar mitzvahs and rabbinical ordination.

In the closing quarter of the twentieth century, Jews were more accepted and increasingly more at ease in America than ever before. The ceilings that had limited their mobility in the earlier part of the 1960s cracked, and Jews became presidents of major universities, including some that at one time had maintained quotas keeping them out, and chief executive officers of corporations, including those that at one time never willingly hired a Jew in any position. Institutions of higher learning that half a century earlier had tried to weed out Jewish applicants now offered courses in Jewish studies and kosher dining facilities.

Yet, in certain segments of American life, anti-Jewish rhetoric rose once again: for example, Jews found themselves the targets of anti-Semitism emanating from elements in the African American community. These verbal attacks and occasional incidents of physical violence terrified Jews, as did the growth of anti-Semitism on the Internet. These unfortunate currents of hate reminded Jews that even here, they might be vulnerable.

Another major theme in the waning decades of the twentieth century was the deep involvement of American Jews with Israel. The year 1967 saw the momentous Six-Day War in Israel, during which Israel captured the West Bank, the Golan Heights, the eastern part of Jerusalem, and Gaza. These controversial events complicated American Jews' relationships with Israel and with each other, dividing them in an angry and anguished discourse.

The Holocaust was still another important theme among American Jews at the end of the twentieth century. Although further removed in time from the horrors of the Holocaust than their parents or grandparents had been,

Women holding Israeli flags march in the New York City Pro-Israeli Parade, 1967. The Six-Day War of 1967 generated an outpouring of emotion from American Jews on behalf of Israel, cementing their bond with the Jewish state.

Jews at the end of the twentieth century found much meaning in this calamitous event.

In short, the Holocaust became a pillar of memory. This emphasis started with Jewish college students in the late 1960s. Many young people took their parents to task for what they considered a lack of political nerve and moral vision during World War II, asserting that American Jews in the 1930s had been complicitous in the Holocaust by not doing enough for their European relatives by confronting American officials.

Some of the earliest public memorializations of the Holocaust took place on college campuses in the late 1960s and early 1970s, when Jewish students organized outdoor candlelight vigils at which they read the names of victims. These college students, often acting under the auspices of Hillel, the organized Jewish presence on campuses, ushered in a new era of Holocaust memorialization. Jewish communities picked up on this momentum, and they, too, began to focus on the Holocaust in new and public ways. Jewish educators designed curricula for children to teach them about the Holocaust, and in 1978, millions of Americans were riveted to their television sets watching the NBC miniseries *Holocaust*.

The following year the memorialization of the Holocaust moved from the private to the official. In 1979 the United States government created a Holocaust Commission, which was subsequently renamed the U.S. Holocaust Memorial Council. In April 1993, after years of deliberation on how the United States could best mark the event, the U.S. Holocaust Memorial Museum opened just steps away from the Mall in Washington, D.C. The imposing building demonstrates not only that Americans have come to view this event as part of their story, but that American Jews had the political and moral influence to bring this about.

The college students who helped launch this Holocaust consciousness also directed their attention to the plight of Jews in the Soviet Union. Just as Holocaust memorialization had existed before student activism, so, too, had quiet discussion among American Jews and Jewish organizations about the brutal suppression of Jewish culture and religion in the Soviet Union. In 1964 five hundred delegates of Jewish organizations got together to form the American Jewish Conference on Soviet Jewry.

But it was the Jewish college students who in 1964 created Student Struggle for Soviet Jewry, which took the movement out of the realm of quiet, behind-the-scenes deliberations to the larger public. Their tactics included marches, rallies, sit-ins, picketing of Soviet consular offices in the United States, and vigils.

The triumph of the movement—the decision of Soviet governments to allow Jewish emigration to Israel, the easing of prohibitions on Jewish observance and education, and ultimately the collapse of the Soviet Union—cannot be attributed to college students. Major international political forces were at work. But without the students' struggle and their activist strategies, Americans would have known little about the issues surrounding the condition of Soviet Jews.

Jewish college students on American campuses could take almost complete credit for another development of this era: the *havurah* movement. *Havurah* means "friendship group." Those who formed such groups saw them as alternatives to established, conventional synagogues. Many Jewish students wanted to be involved in religious ritual but did not like the rabbi-dominated practice of American Judaism. Neither did they like the emphasis on decorum and orderliness. Finally, many *havurah* members did not like the gendered hierarchy that pervaded even Reform synagogues.

So both on campuses and in cities such as Boston, New York, and Washington *havurot* were formed. These groups had no rabbis—although some members might have been ordained rabbis—and usually lacked a building. They might meet in apartments or in rented spaces. Members might come wearing blue jeans, and in some *havurot* they removed their shoes before worship. They could often be found sitting on the floor or reclining on cushions rather than sitting primly in elegantly carved pews.

Everybody in the *havurah* played a role in leading services, reading Torah, and moderating discussions, and therefore many boundaries that defined synagogue life were erased. Members in some *havurot* innovated with interpretive dance and sometimes incorporated meditation and readings from Eastern religions. They took Judaism seriously, and they took seriously their right and responsibility to enhance its practice.

The *havurah* movement inspired creative use of music. Some members became fascinated with east European Jewish melodies, *nigunim*, and with the Jewish musical styles of Russia and Poland associated with the *klezmer* musicians, who played at weddings in Jewish communities. Others turned to the graphic arts, creating innovative ritual objects characterized by the bright colors and abstract images dominating the counterculture. Some rediscovered the Jewish art of papercutting, a form that had died out in America.

Movie still from Schindler's List, *1991.* Schindler's List, *the story of a German industrialist who uses his factory to save hundreds of Jews during the Holocaust, was a critical and commercial success. Stephen Spielberg, the most successful director in the history of American film, won his first Academy Award for his work.*

The influence of the *havurot* spilled out beyond the New York Havurah, Boston's Havurat Shalom, or Washington's Fabrangen. Rabbis, denominational bodies, and the lay members of the synagogues saw the kind of dynamism and energy being created in the *havurah* movement and tried to incorporate some of its elements into more conventional synagogue life, thus the new attention to art, music, and dance spread from the confines of the *havurot* into the more mainstream American Jewish cultural repertoire.

The *havurah* movement also had a powerful effect on women's role in religious observance. In the *havurot,* women for the first time played a role equal to that of men, and this was empowering. Indeed, this change was one of the revolutionary developments in American Judaism that grew out of this period and the ferment that originated on college campuses.

In the spring of 1972, most American Jews were surprised to learn that among the graduates of Hebrew Union College (HUC) who received their rabbinic ordination was a woman, Sally Preisand. Perhaps they should not have been surprised, since the issue had been in the air for a while. For example, in 1968, the Reconstructionist Rabbinical College had (RRC) opened in Philadelphia, announcing that women were welcome to apply and that their ordination as rabbis would be no issue whatsoever. RRC's bold decision, Preisand's ordination, the hundreds of women who followed her at HUC, and the ferment of women's involvement with the *havurot* opened the floodgate for women to enter the rabbinic structure.

In 1972, the call for admitting women to Conservative Judaism's rabbinical program at the Jewish Theological Seminary came from a group of women, called Ezrat Nashim, many of whom had been deeply influenced by the *havurah* movement and the feminist movement. Ezrat Nashim brought its first demand to the meeting of the Rabbinical Assembly, and, more than a decade later, in May 1985, Amy Eilberg became the first woman to receive ordination at the Jewish Theological Seminary.

Besides this dramatic series of developments that began in the late 1960s —the sacralization of the Holocaust, the militancy of the Soviet Jewry

movement, the innovations in ritual and worship, and the advances of women—Jewish learning also transformed in this period. Until the late 1960s very little in the way of Jewish studies existed in American universities. Just a handful of courses were taught by a few individual professors. The study of the Jewish experience, past and present, played no role in the academic programs of American colleges. Thus, most students were unable to seriously study Jewish history, culture, literature, or philosophy in an American university. (Brandeis University, which had been founded in 1948, was an exception.)

This all changed in the late 1960s. Jewish students began to ask for such courses. Professors who had an interest in the subject began to teach them. Individuals in the Jewish communities with financial means offered funding to colleges and universities, both public and private, to hire professors to teach these subjects. Moreover, the demand for faculty to teach Jewish history, Jewish literature, and Jewish philosophy led students to pursue Jewish studies at the graduate level, which in turn fostered the growth of the field and the number of courses, programs, departments, conferences, scholarly books, and journals devoted to the subject.

College students holding a candlelight vigil honoring Russian Jews, 1969. The movement to assist Soviet Jewry emerged in the early 1960s, in response to rising anti-Semitism and Soviet emigration restrictions on Jews. Jewish students employed the tactics of the Civil Rights movement on behalf of this cause.

This same kind of attention led communities and donors to create Jewish
day schools, private Jewish schools that divided the day between secular
subjects and Judaic subjects, including Hebrew language, Bible, rabbinics,
and Jewish history. Until the late 1960s the vast majority of American
Jewish children received their education in public schools and relied on
afternoon or Sunday schools for their Jewish education. Even among the
Orthodox, before the mid- to late-1960s, public school education was the
rule, and Jews were among some of its staunchest supporters.

This educational change was based on nearly universal American Jewish
affluence and acceptance. In previous decades, few Jews could afford private
education, and they were too uncomfortable in America, too nervous about
the way non-Jews viewed them, to enroll their children in all-Jewish
schools. In the last decades of the twentieth century, however, Jews had
achieved economic prosperity. They also were so thoroughly American, and
their Americanness was so unquestionably accepted by others, that they felt
they could afford the luxury of intensive Jewish education.

At the same time a big issue in the Jewish communal agenda at the end of the twentieth century was the concern about whether Jewishness could be sustained in any significant way into the next century. Denominations and synagogues struggled with this matter in their own ways. And pockets of anti-Semitism continued to exist. Many still viewed Jews as alien, as out-siders in a Christian nation, and as powerfully evil people who exploit the poor. This rhetoric emanated from two sectors: the religious Right and por-tions of the African American community.

In the late 1970s, the rise of the religious right challenged the belief that America was a country of many religious communities and that people's reli-gious choices were private. Christian fundamentalists asserted in political campaigns and radio and television shows that the nation was a Christian one and that its moral fiber had declined ever since secular values had taken root.

The traditional lighting of candles on Friday evenings is still regarded as one of the major markers of Jewish identity.

Rabbi Sally Priesand, the first practicing woman rabbi, 1972. The first female candidate to apply for ordination from Hebrew Union College was Martha Neumark, in 1924. The Board of Governors rejected her application. Photo: © Bettmann/CORBIS.

Also, since the end of the 1960s, American Jews had found themselves involved in a string of confrontations with African Americans. First, Black activists in the freedom struggle demanded that Jews leave the movement, and this was a sad moment. Jews had taken tremendous pride in their involvement in civil rights, and they took the Black Power movement as a rejection of their historical involvement with the struggle for a better America.

Second, in the late 1960s, large-scale riots took place in many American cities—Newark, Detroit, Cleveland, Washington, Chicago, and Los Angeles—after the assassination of Martin Luther King, Jr., in April 1968. Much of the violence, which was an outgrowth of poverty and the unfulfilled promises of the era of civil rights, was directed at white-owned businesses in the Black neighborhoods of these cities. An inordinate number of these stores' proprietors were Jews, many of them older people who had owned these grocery stores, furniture stores, clothing shops, dry cleaners, and liquor stores for decades. To the Jews who operated these shops, the riots spelled the end of their enterprises.

The riots also caused Jews who still lived in the inner cities, and who were usually poor, to join the Jewish majority in the suburbs. After the riots, few Jews were left within the city limits of Newark and Detroit. The suburban trend that had begun after World War II was nearly complete.

Third, Jews and Blacks differed over a series of political issues, particularly matters of affirmative action and how best to redress the inequities that had become structurally embedded in American life. Although neither community was homogeneous in its views, Jews were almost universally appalled

*Senator Joseph Lieberman,
Democrat from Connecticut,
being interviewed on
NBC's "Meet the Press,"
June 10, 2001.*

at the rhetoric of Louis Farrakhan, a leader of the Nation of Islam, who described Judaism to enormous crowds of African Americans as a "gutter religion." Others from the Nation of Islam blamed Jewish doctors for the AIDS epidemic, and claimed that Jews were responsible for slavery.

In the summer of 1991 a tragic event occurred in Brooklyn's Crown Heights neighborhood. A little boy, a Black child, was accidentally run over by an automobile driven by a Hasid. In this mixed Black and Jewish neighborhood, where almost all the Jews were Hasidim, rioting broke out. Bands of Black teenagers terrorized the local Hasidic population. Many of the Hasidim were the children of Holocaust survivors, and the images that flashed in their minds were of Nazis and pogroms.

Fortunately, by the end of the twentieth century the Black-Jewish rift seemed dormant. Religious and political representatives of the two groups had begun to find more ways to work together to explore issues of common concern rather than emphasize differences that separate them.

American life and culture at the end of the twentieth century, its movies and books, its courts and legislatures, its universities and newspaper, its concert halls and corporations, were places where Jews left their mark. Indeed no book could be long enough to list the incredible number of American Jews who helped shape American culture, politics, and society at the end of the twentieth century.

Jewish Day School, Merion Station, Pennsylvania. A major development in the American Jewish world since the 1960s, across the denominational spectrum, has been the Jewish day school movement. Photo: David H. Wells/CORBIS.

Perhaps symbolically we can point to the nomination of Joseph Lieberman. Lieberman, an Orthodox Jew, joined the Democratic Party's 2000 national ticket as their vice presidential candidate. While Lieberman did not become vice president, the nomination and campaign had great meaning for American Jews, clear evidence of their arrival at the center of American life.

Twelve American Jews won Nobel Prizes in economics between 1970 and 1999. These men—Paul Samuelson, Robert Solow, Herbert Simon,

Bella Abzug casts her vote in New York City's primary election, 1977. Bella Abzug graduated from Columbia Law School, after which she battled fiercely in court as a labor and civil rights lawyer. In 1961 she was one of the founders of Women's Strike for Peace, and in 1970 she was elected to the U.S. House of Representatives. Photo: UPI/Corbis-Bettmann.

Kenneth Arrow, Gary Becker, Robert Fogel, Milton Friedman, Joshn Harsanyi, Lawrence Klein, Simon Kuznets, Herbert Miller, and Harry Mordowitz—helped Americans understand the nature of the economic system and made it possible to plan for the future. In doing so, they are joined by Alan Greenspan, the head of the Federal Reserve Board, thought by many to be the architect of the prosperity of the 1990s.

Chemistry, biology, mathematics, medicine, and physics were fields that attracted Jewish students and in which Jews helped to shape the contours of knowledge. Murray Gell-Mann won the Nobel Prize for physics in

A Bar Mitzvah, Seattle, Washington, 1970. Although most bar and bat mitzvahs are celebrated on Saturdays, they may first be observed during the week, closer to the actual date of the child's Hebrew birthday. Photo: © Ted Spiegel/CORBIS.

Lubavitcher Jews praying, Borough Park, Brooklyn, New York, c. 1990. Although they are but one of many sects of Hasidim, the Lubavitch are by far the best known. They have actively worked to recruit new followers and publicly promote Judaism. Photo: © Catherine Karnow/CORBIS.

A Jewish diamond cutter examines a stone before cutting it, New York, 1984. Orthodox Jews play an important role in the diamond industry in Europe, America, and Israel. In New York, they are a highly visible presence in the diamond district, on 47th Street. Photo: © Bettmann/CORBIS.

1969 with his discovery of the "Quark" theory, and Sheldon Glashow won in 1979 for his work on unified weak and electromagnetic interactions between elementary particles. The list of Jewish winners of the Nobel Prize and other coveted awards in the sciences deserves a book of its own!

In the 1990s two Jews were named to the Supreme Court. Ruth Bader Ginsburg had been an architect of legal victories for women in the 1970s and 1980s, and an outspoken advocate for civil rights for all Americans. She was joined on the Court by Stephen Breyer, and these two justices held up the liberal end of the U.S. Supreme Court.

The feminist movement that has transformed America in the last part of the twentieth century was aided not just by Ruth Bader Ginsburg's legal strategies but by the writing and activism of other Jews. In 1963, Betty Friedan wrote *The Feminine Mystique*, the book that launched the women's movement. She was aided in her work by Gloria Steinem, who founded *Ms. Magazine*, and Andrea Dworkin, one of the movement's theoreticians.

Jewish jounalists and nationally syndicated columnists help inform the American public about the great issues of the day. Anthony Lewis, David Broder, Thomas Friedman, Ellen Goodman, and Richard Cohen are just a

Federal Reserve Chairman Alan Greenspan appears before Congress's Joint Economic committee to testify about the economy, 1997. Greenspan, appointed by President Reagan as chairman of the Federal Reserve in 1987, is among the most powerful and widely recognized American officials, both internationally and domestically.

few of these print journalists whose words shape public opinion. In academia in every field—history, sociology, anthropology, literature, philosophy, classics, political science—Jewish professors and scholars educate America's students and produce the scholarship that changes our understanding of society and culture, past and present. Fields that were once off-limits to Jews are now comfortable intellectual homes for them. Indeed, one of the notable turns of the 1980s and beyond was that Jews became the presidents of Harvard, Yale, Princeton, Dartmouth, Columbia, the University of Chicago, the University of Pennsylvania, and Williams College, many of these being colleges that once sought to keep Jews out.

And as mentioned in earlier chapters, Jews of the twentieth century have contributed greatly to the arts and culture. Some of the writers who started out in the 1950s, like Saul Bellow and Philip Roth, were still writing best-sellers at the beginning of the twenty-first century. They were joined by, among others, such novelists as E. L. Doctorow, Allegra Maud Goodman, Rebecca Goldstein, Paul Auster, and Judy Blume, all of whom contributed to a corpus of books that we call "American literature."

Likewise in the realm of popular culture, American Jews continued to entertain people around the world. Woody Allen, Barbra Streisand, Neil Simon, Mandy Patinkin, Neil Diamond, Natalie Portman, Richard Dreyfus, Andy Bergman, Wendy Wasserstein, Jerry Seinfeld, Stephen Spielberg, and Goldie Hawn constitute just the tip of the entertainment iceberg. They, along with Jews in the fashion industry, Calvin Klein, Ralph Lauren, Isaac Mizrahi, and Donna Karan, have created a range of beautiful and stylish products that the world consumes.

Far left: *Before she was appointed to the Supreme Court in 1993, Ruth Bader Ginsberg's posts included head of the ACLU's Women's Rights Project and the first tenured female professor of law at Columbia University.*

Left: *Robert Morris Morgenthau has enjoyed distinction as a public official for several decades. He has served as the District Attorney of New York County*

A CLOSER LOOK:
ENTERTAINMENT

Where would today's entertainment industry be without the likes of Stephen Spielberg, Mel Brooks, Woody Allen, Barbra Streisand, Dustin Hoffman, Wendy Wasserstein, and Neil Simon? These and countless other Jewish Americans—performers, directors, business-people, and decision-makers who have chosen to make entertainment their life's work—have helped shape the way Americans view themselves, each other, and the world.

Left: Film producer and director Stephen Spielberg with his Oscars for Best Director and Best Picture at the Academy Awards, Los Angeles, 1994.

Below: Mel Brooks seated on a camera crane, directing the film Silent Movie, *c. 1976.*

Opposite, top left: Goldie Hawn, seen here as Private Benjamin *(1980), has become one of Hollywood's most sought-after comic actresses.*

Opposite, top right: Woody Allen, pictured in 1970, has achieved tremendous success writing, directing, and acting the part of America's favorite neurotic.

Opposite, below: Gene Wilder played a Polish rabbi who makes a hilarious cross-country trip to San Francisco in The Frisco Kid, *1979.*

Opposite, top left: *Barbra Streisand with her Cecil B. DeMille award, at the Golden Globe Awards.*

Opposite, top right: *Playwright Neil Simon with his favorite "Odd Couple," Walter Matthau and Jack Lemmon.*

Opposite, bottom: *Wendy Wasserstein celebrating her Pulitzer Prize for The Heidi Chronicles. Photo: © CORBIS.*

Above: *Nathan Lane and Matthew Broderick join other stars in support for Broadway and tourism after the tragedy of September 11, 2001.*

Left: *Actors Mandy Patinkin and Bernadette Peters, with composer Stephen Sondheim. Photo: ©Bettmann/CORBIS.*

Lenny Krayzelburg after receiving his gold medal for winning the 100-meter backstroke at the Pan Pacific Championships, Sydney, Australia, August 1999. Despite their reputation as intellectuals, American Jews have also distinguished themselves in sports.

One area in which American Jews have only recently become more visible is sports. One has only to look at the results of Olympic competition over the past thirty years to appreciate their contribution. Medal winners from Mark Spitz to Mitch Gaylord to Lenny Krayzelburg have proudly saluted the American flag.

American popular culture would not be the same without the talents and energies of the American Jewish women and men who are at one and the same time, artists, Americans, and Jews. Sometimes their art directly reflects their experiences as Jews. Sometimes it does not. Either way the opportunities America has offered and the creative talents Jews have displayed enrich the lives of all Americans.

As the new millennium begins, the story of the Jewish Americans is far from over. What has come to a close for many, however, is their search for a place to end their wanderings.

A CLOSER LOOK:
ISAAC STERN

The American violinist Isaac Stern was born in the Ukraine in 1920 and was brought to San Francisco as an infant. His mother was a pianist and music teacher, and she gave him his first music lessons. Like a number of other Jewish violinists—Jascha Heifitz, Yehudi Menuhin, and Efrem Zimbalist—Isaac Stern debuted as a child and demonstrated his musical brilliance at a young age. By eleven he was the violin soloist with the San Francisco Orchestra. His broader reputation soared after World War II, and Isaac Stern went on to bring music to people all over the country and the world. An activist as well as a spectacular performer, Stern helped organize the effort to save Carnegie Hall from demolition.

An active participant in worldwide Jewish musical culture, Stern has been associated with the Israeli music establishment as well. He appeared frequently with the Israel Philharmonic, established programs to help gifted music students in Israel pursue their studies, and when in the 1990s massive immigration to Israel from the Soviet Union began, Stern created a number of programs to help launch the musical careers in Israel of the many young Russian musicians who had had to uproot themselves.

A CLOSER LOOK:
FASHION

Several Jewish clothing designers are among the most influential forces that have dressed fashionable Americans—and their names are among the most recognizable in the realm of fashion.

With his own take on all-American casual wear, as well as nine lines of perfume, **Calvin Klein** has carved out a huge estate in the world of fashion. Born in 1942 and educated at New York's High School of Art and Design and the Fashion Institute of Technology, Klein was immediately recognized for the simple, clean lines of his early collections in the 1960s. In 1993 he received an award as America's Best Designer, and *Time* magazine has named him one of America's 25 most influential people.

Above: *Calvin Klein at the presentation of his 2001 fall/winter collection in New York City.*

Left: *Isaac Mizrahi takes a bow at the conclusion of his fall 1998 fashion show in New York City.*

Opposite, above: *Donna Karan at the Metropolitan Museum of Art in New York City, attending the opening of an exhibit that pays tribute to designer Christian Dior.*

Opposite, below: *Ralph Lauren at the conclusion of his fall 1997 fashion show in New York City.*

Ralph Lauren (born Ralph Lifshitz in 1939) founded Polo Fashions New York in 1968, but his fame really skyrocketed when he designed the male costumes for the 1974 film version of *The Great Gatsby,* starring Robert Redford and Mia Farrow. Ralph Lauren was the first designer to sell a complete look—a quintessential successful American "lifestyle"—rather than just an article of clothing. The Council of Fashion Designers of America (CFDA) honored him with a Lifetime Achievement Award in 1992.

Isaac Mizrahi was born in Brooklyn, and studied at a local yeshiva for eight years. Even then, he was creating fashion sketches in the pages of his prayer book, and making original clothing for his mother's friends. He introduced his own line of fashion in 1987, and won recognition from

CFDA as Designer of the Year twice, before Chanel stopped funding his design efforts. An effervescent personality, Mizrahi has appeared in several movies, including a documentary of his life titled *Unzipped* (1995) and a stage production called *Les MIZrahi* (2000).

The cards were stacked to send **Donna Karan** into the world of fashion. Born in Queens, New York, she grew up with a step-father who was a tailor, and a mother who was a model. She worked for Liz Claiborne while still in school, and designed for Anne Klein for ten years, before founding her own company in 1985. Her "Essentials" line, based on a system of interchangeable pieces that work together to create a wardrobe, made Karan known for a style that melded simplicity and practicality with attractiveness. Later, her moderately priced, accessible DKNY brand expanded her popularity to a broader audience. Called the "Queen of Seventh Avenue," Karan has earned an unequaled six CFDA awards for design excellence, and has organized a broad array of charitable events.

A CLOSER LOOK:
CHARITY

Charity is not just a good idea, a Jew's bumper sticker might tell you, it's the law. The giving of *tzedakah* to the less fortunate is mandated in the Torah, and for centuries, Jewish communities around the world have maintained a collection box, or *kuppah*, to which everyone make regular contributions. This collection has funded a broad variety of welfare projects, from feeding the hungry and sheltering the homeless, to providing dowries for poor girls, to burying the dead.

When Jews came to America, the concept of *tzedakah* came with them. After some had begun to prosper in the major cities—New York, Boston, Philadelphia, Chicago, Baltimore—they made it a priority to look after their less fortunate co-religionists, paving the way for more Jews to build comfortable lives in America.

While philanthropy began as the work of individuals—many but not all of them wealthy—it soon became a centralized community effort. The local fundraising groups in Boston joined together under

the aegis of the Combined Jewish Philanthropies, and other cities quickly followed their lead, forming federations of their own to look after immigrants' health, vocational education, child care needs, and community development.

Societies such as the Hebrew Free Loan Society and the Hebrew Immigrant Aid Society were among the most widely influential. The Hebrew Free Loan Society gave a $250 loan to any Jewish immigrant in need, requiring no collateral but a signature, trusting that when the borrower prospered, the loan would be repaid. Only two people ever failed to repay this loan—one because he died before he could afford to pay it back. All the rest were able to establish sufficient income to support themselves and their families, given this initial boost. Meanwhile, the Hebrew Immigrant Aid Society (HIAS), founded in New York by Russian and eastern European Jews, offered food, shelter, transportation, jobs, and other assistance to an incredible number of new arrivals.

Today, there are hundreds of Jewish charitable organizations. The largest of these is the United Jewish Communities (formerly United Jewish Appeal), which raises money for Jews in need everywhere, throughout the world. Their partner is the Joint Distribution Committee, the "overseas arm of the American Jewish community," performing relief and rescue missions in troubled parts of the world. HIAS still exists, and has helped more than 4.5 million refugees from around the world in their quest to escape persecution and privation.

American Jews also contribute to organizations founded in other countries, such as the Jewish National Fund, which is dedicated to purchasing and "redeeming" land in Israel, and ORT, which provides vocational training to Jews who need it.

Opposite: *Invitation to a Fancy Dress Ball of the Purim Association of the City of New York, 1881, which was founded in 1862 to sponsor annual costume balls for "the relief of the necessities of others."*

Above: *Temple Emanu-El charity dinner held at The Plaza, New York City, 1944.*

Right: *Designer Donna Karan announces a national campaign, "Fashion for America: Shop to show your support," after the attack of September 11, 2001. The proceeds from the sale of the T-shirt she wears went to the relief funds.*

Below: *A little girl follows the tradition of charity to others by placing a contribution in her tzedakah box.*

CFDA / VOGUE

JEWISH SITES ON THE INTERNET

COMPREHENSIVE and GENERAL SITES:

1. The Jewish Virtual Library
http://www.us-israel.org/jsource/
The most comprehensive online Jewish encyclopedia in the world, with more than 6,000 articles and 2,000 photographs and maps. The Library has 13 wings: History, Women, The Holocaust, Travel, Israel & The States, Maps, Politics, Biography, Israel, Religion, Judaic Treasures of the Library of Congress, Vital Statistics and Reference. Each of these has numerous subcategories.

2. Shamash: The Jewish Network
http://www.shamash.org
This site strives to be the highest quality central point of Jewish information and discussion on the Internet. It features a book of the week, a national directory of kosher restaurants, and a collection of links larger than the one you're reading now.

3. MavenSearch
http://www.maven.co.il
With little content of its own, this "portal to the Jewish world" is a directory and search engine focusing on Jewish information.

4. About.com: Judaism
http://judaism.about.com
A variety of content, including an Introduction to Judaism, Jewish Holiday Calendar, and Jewish recipes and "how-to" pages. Also includes links related to Judaism.

5. BBC Online: Judaism
http://www.bbc.co.uk/religion/religions/judaism/
Overview of Judaism, including history, beliefs, customs, and holy days.

6. Jewish Community Online
http://www.jewish.com
This site aims to provide unique, useful and engaging information for and about the American Jewish community. They maintain community areas including "ask the rabbi"; reference tools, including a complete electronic translation of the Torah, and over 7,000 non-commercial Jewish web links.

JEWISH HISTORY and ART:

7. Learning about the Holocaust through Art
http://www.holocaust-education.net
The primary goal of this project is to create a significant, high-quality resource about the art of the Holocaust for researchers, educators, students and the wider public.

8. Gateway to Sephardic Resources
http://www.bsz.org
This site focuses on the history and culture of Sephardic Jews—those whose ancestors came from Spain and Portugal.

9. The Jewish Museum, New York
http://www.jewishmuseum.org
The largest Jewish museum in the western hemisphere.

10. The Israel Museum, Jerusalem
http://www.imj.org.il
The Israel Museum was founded in 1965 and has, in a remarkably short period of time, become the encylopedic museum of art and archeology for that part of the world.

11. Jewish Art Network
http://www.jewishartnetwork.com
Jewish Art Network features artwork from the Vilna Gaon Jewish Museum in Vilnius and from private Jewish artists throughout the world. All digitalized images in our gallery may be enlarged to full-screen size. Whenever possible, information about a given artist and his work will also be included.

12. American Jewish Historical Society
http://www.ajhs.org
The mission of the AJHS is to foster awareness and appreciation of the American Jewish past and to serve as a national scholarly resource for research through the collection, preservation and dissemination of materials relating to American Jewish history.

13. Internet Jewish History Sourcebook
http://www.fordham.edu/halsall/jewish/jewishbook.html
Historical texts with a Jewish perspective, from the emergence of Judaism through the Middle Ages, the Enlightenment, and beyond.

14. **Jewish History Resource Center**
http://www.hum.huji.ac.il/Dinur/
Over 6,000 documents in over 30 categories relating to Jewish history, selected and organized by the staff of the Hebrew University of Jerusalem.

JEWISH LAW and CUSTOM:

15. **Navigating the Bible**
http://bible.ort.org
The complete Torah online, in Hebrew, English, and English transliteration, with commentary. Also features RealAudio sound clips to demonstrate the chanting of every verse.

16. **Project Genesis**
http://www.torah.org
This site is devoted to education on all aspects of Jewish tradition. Features Torah portions, archived essays, online classes, and other Jewish educational material.

17. **Kashrut.com**
http://www.kashrut.com
The premier kosher information source on the web.

18. **Judaism 101**
http://www.jewfaq.org
An "online encyclopedia of Judaism," organized as a very complete set of Frequently Asked Questions.

19. **Glossary of Basic Jewish Terms and Concepts**
http://www.ou.org/about/judaism.htm
Provides authoritative definitions of Jewish terms, from A to Z.

20. **Jewish Torah Audio**
http://www.613.org
Classes, stories, sermons, and songs—hours of downloadable Jewish audio, in RealAudio format. Requires free RealPlayer software (and a fast Internet connection doesn't hurt, either).

21. **Shiur.net**
http://www.shiur.net
This site's goal is to bring the Torah of the Yeshiva University *Rabbeim*, in streaming audio format, into your home.

22. **Virtual Beit Midrash**
http://www.vbm-torah.org
Providing yeshiva style lessons in Torah and Judaism to students of all ages, outside the yeshiva walls. Courses are sent out, and instructors are accessible, via e-mail. There is also a large archive of past articles.

23. **Just Tzedakah: Information on charitable giving**
http://www.just-tzedakah.org
Guidelines for Jewish law and thought on the subject of charity. Profiles of specific Jewish charities, and online opportunities for giving.

24. **Everything Jewish**
http://www.everythingjewish.com
Despite its name, this site seems to focus mainly on historical discussion of the holidays.

JEWISH ORGANIZATIONS:

25. **World Jewish Congress**
http://www.wjc.org.il
An international federation of Jewish communities and organizations. As an umbrella group it represents Jews from the entire political spectrum and from all Jewish religious denominations, serving as a diplomatic arm of the Jewish people to world governments and international organizations.

26. **American Jewish Congress**
http://www.ajcongress.org
A major political activist organization that acts in accordance with Jewish interests and ideals.

27. **American ORT**
http://www.aort.org
ORT's mission is to provide technological education to communities in industrialized countries. ORT is the Jewish world's leader in technology education and the world's largest non-governmental education and training organization.

28. **National Jewish Coalition for Literacy**
http://www.njcl.net
America's Jews share a common heritage of a love for books and the written word, a commitment to quality education, and a passion for the pursuit of social justice. Based on this historical legacy, the NJCL believes that

our community is well positioned to play an important role in the effort to promote literacy.

29. United Jewish Communities
http://www.ujc.org
The largest Jewish charitable organization in America, the UJC raises money for Jews in need everywhere, throughout the world.

30. Joint Distribution Committee
http://www.jdc.org
The overseas arm of the American Jewish community, the JDC performs relief and rescue missions in troubled parts of the world. The JDC is funded primarily by the United Jewish Communities.

31. Hebrew Immigrant Aid Society
http://www.hias.org
Founded in 1881, HIAS has offered food, shelter, transportation, jobs, and other assistance to more than four and a half million people in need of rescue, reunion, and resettlement.

32. Jewish National Fund
http://www.jnf.org
This "caretaker of the land of Israel" is dedicated to purchasing and "redeeming" land in Israel.

33. Anti-Defamation League
http://www.adl.org
For more than 88 years, ADL has been combating anti-Semitism and bigotry of all kinds.

DENOMINATIONS:

34. Reform Judaism
http://rj.org
An overview of the Reform movement, maintained by the Union of American Hebrew Congregations.

35. Hebrew Union College
http://huc.edu
The academic arm of the Reform movement.

36. United Synagogue of Conservative Judaism
http://www.uscj.org
The association of Conservative congregations in North America, today consisting of 800 affiliated synagogues and over one-and-a-half-million members.

37. Jewish Theological Seminary
http://www.jtsa.edu
The academic arm of the Conservative movement.

38. Rabbinical Council of America
http://www.rabbis.org
A dynamic professional organization serving over 1,100 Orthodox Rabbis. The Council serves as a spokesman for Orthodoxy on the national and international level.

JEWISH NEWS:

39. Virtual Jerusalem
http://www.virtualjerusalem.com
An online newspaper (in English) focusing on Israeli themes. Lots of content, frequently updated.

40. Ha'aretz: English Edition
http://www.haaretzdaily.com
An independent daily newspaper in Israel, with a broadly liberal outlook both on domestic issues and on international affairs. The paper is perhaps best known for its Op-ed page, where its senior columnists reflect on current events.

41. JTA: Global Jewish News
http://www.jta.org
JTA is an international news service, based in New York, that provides up-to-the-minute reports, analysis pieces and features on events and issues of concern to the Jewish people.

42. The Forward
http://www.forward.com
An important weekly Jewish publication, launched in 1897.

MISCELLANEOUS:

43. JewishGen
http://www.jewishgen.org
The primary source for Jewish genealogy on the web.

44. Mispacha: for Jewish Families
http://www.mishpacha.org
Mishpacha is for parents who find that what they learned

as Jewish children isn't enough to build their own Jewish families. A starting point for a spiritual journey, the site provides guideposts to Jewish belief, practice and community.

45. **Jewz.com**
http://www.jewz.com
A hip, lifestyle- and entertainment-oriented site for a Jewish audience.

46. **Harry Leichter's Jewish Humor**
http://www.haruth.com/jhumorlink.htm
Extensive landmark collection of Jewish jokes, humorous items, and links.

47. **Jewish calendar software for Windows**
http://www.tichnut.de/jewish/
This Jewish calendar software has many valuable features. There used to be a Macintosh version on this site, too—it appears to have been discontinued.

48. **PilotYid: Jewish Software for PalmOS**
http://www.pilotyid.com
PilotYid is a collection of Jewish and Hebrew-related software for any PDA that runs the Palm OS Computing® Platform.

49. **Excerpts from our other Judaica books**
http://www.HLLA.com/reference/index.html#judaica
Levin Associates (the publisher of this book) publishes a broad—and ever-expanding—variety of books on Jewish themes and Jewish art. Excerpts from many of these books are available on our web site.

50. **Hugh Lauter Levin Associates Jewish Links**
http://www.HLLA.com/reference/jewishlinks.html
The list of links from this very book is on the publisher's web site (at *http://www.HLLA.com*), so that if you don't want to type in all these links (or carry the book around with you), you can go to our page and click on any of them.

INDEX

Page numbers in *italics* refer to illustrations.

PHOTO CREDITS

Courtesy American Jewish Archives: pp. 28, 55, 56, 67, 70, 86 (top and bottom), 117, 120 (above), 122-123, 143, 161.

Courtesy American Jewish Historical Society, Waltham, Massachusetts, and New York, New York: pp. 30, 45, 53, 58, 60, 63, 72, 91, 107, 118 (below, left), 129 (left), 135, 138 (both), 144, 148, 160, 168, 174, 178, 195, 207, 230, 231 (above).

Archive Photos: pp. 27, 154, 170, 183 (above), 184 (both), 185, 186 (above), 188, 192 (left), 192 (below) (R. Dumont), 193 (top), 193 (bottom) (Columbia), 202 (Bernard Gottfryd), 205 (Universal Pictures/Fotos International), 219 (Reuters/Mike Theiler), 220, 221 (left) (Bernard Gottfryd), 221 (below) (Jim Bourg/Reuters), 222 (left) (Reuters/Blake Sell), 222 (below) (Popperfoto), 223 (top, left), 223 (top, right) (Gerald Davis), 224 (top, right) (copyright 1998 Paramount Pictures Corp.), 226 (Reuters), 228 (left) (Reuters/Brad Rickerby), 229 (top) (Reuters/Mike Segar), 229 (bottom) (Reuters/Peter Morgan); George Eastman House: p. 133; copyright 2001 Getty Images: pp. 15 (Spencer Platt/Newsmakers), 211 (Alex Wong), 221 (far left) (Liaison), 225 (above) (George De Sota), 228 (above) (Arnaldo Magnini/Liaison), 231 (right) (Mario Tama); Hulton Getty Collection: pp. 99, 151 (below, left) (Liaison), 155 (all), 157 (top, left), 157 (bottom), 157 (top, right) (Baron Collection), 173 (Sporting News), 179 (Jim Wells), 181 (Jim Wells), 182, 186 (below) (Eric Auerbach), 189, 190 (both), 191 (top, right), 223 (bottom) (Warner Bros.), 224 (top, left), 227 (both); Museum of the City of New York: p. 151 (below, right).

Arizona Historical Society, Tucson: pp. 124, 131 (below).

Bill Aron Photography: pp. 197, 208.

Art Resource: The Andy Warhol Foundation, Inc.: pp. 13, 159; The Jewish Museum, New York: p. 26; Scala: pp. 8-9.

Courtesy The Autry Museum of Western Heritage, Los Angeles, Courtesy of Andrea Kalinowski: p. 127 (bottom quilt).

Courtesy The Bancroft Library, University of California, Berkeley: pp. 74, 126 (right quilt photo) (Auerback Family photograph collection #000393).

Courtesy Beck Archives, Special Collection at Penrose Library, Rocky Mountain Jewish Historical Society, Denver: p. 128.

Bettmann/CORBIS: front cover, pp. 34, 105, 114 (right), 116, 118 (above and left), 136, 151 (right), 156, 158 (left), 158 (right) (U.S. Navy Photo from United Press), 170-171 (background), 171, 172 (above), 183 (left), 191 (top, left), 191 (bottom), 194, 200, 210, 212, 213, 214-215. 216-217, 218, 224 (bottom), 225 (left).

Courtesy Boston Public Library: p. 149.

Published with Permission of Congregation Beth Elohim, Charleston, South Carolina, and The McKissick Museum: p. 62.

Courtesy Shai Ginott: p. 23.

Courtesy The Hadassah Archives, New York: p. 172 (below).

David Harris: p. 24.

Courtesy Dr. Albert Holstein: p. 139.

John Hopf Photography: pp. 44, 49.

HUC Skirball Museum: p. 141 (both); pp. 6, 89, 140, back cover (John Reed Forsman); pp. 11, 162 (Susan Einstein).

Israel Museum, Jerusalem: pp. 19, 21.

Courtesy Jewish Historical Society of the Upper Midwest, St. Paul, Minnesota, p. 175.

The Jewish Museum of Maryland: p. 85.

Courtesy of The Jewish National Fund: p. 167.

Courtesy The Library of the Jewish Theological Seminary of America: pp. 29, 81 (Suzanne Kaufman).

The Kansas State Historical Society, Topeka: p. 64.

Courtesy of Abraham and Deborah Karp: p. 88.

Library of Congress: pp. 32-33, 39, 41, 42, 73, 82, 103, 110, 112 (right and below), 114 (left: top, middle, bottom), 129 (above), 146, 165.

Courtesy Rita F. Malkin: pp. 98, 169.

Copyright 1986 The Metropolitan Museum of Art: p. 54 (Schecter Lee).

Minnesota Historical Society: p. 137 (Norton & Peel).

The Museum of the City of New York: p. 111 (The Byron Collection).

Nahum Goldman Museum of the Jewish Diaspora, Beth Hatefutsoth Photo Archive, Courtesy of Zusia Efron Collection, Tel Aviv, Israel: p. 97.

Collection of The New-York Historical Society: pp. 38, 100-101, 126 (left quilt, bottom photos) (left: #74487) (right: #50593).

The New York Public Library: p. 102; Picture Collection: pp. 108, 130; U.S. History Division, Print Collection, Miriam and Ira D. Wallach Division of Art, Print and Photographs, Astor, Lenox and Tilden Foundations: p. 43.

Richard T. Nowitz: pp. 198, 201, 209.

Opera News Archives, Francis Robinson Collection: p. 12.

The Ida Pearle and Joseph Cuba Archives of the William Berman Jewish Heritage Museum: p. 92.

Philadelphia Jewish Archives Center at The Balch Institute, Philadelphia: p. 113.

Seaver Center for Western History Research, Natural History Museum of Los Angeles County: pp. 108-109.

Courtesy Shearith Israel Congregation: p. 37.

Smith College Museum of Art: p. 176 (Stephen Petegorsky).

Smithsonian Institution, Washington, D.C.: p. 118 (below, right).

Spertus Institute of Jewish Studies, Chicago Jewish Archives: p. 96.

Courtesy The State Historical Society of North Dakota, "Early Days: The Story of Sarah Thal, Wife of a Pioneer Farmer of Nelson County, North Dakota": p. 127 (top quilt).

Courtesy Levi Strauss & Co., San Francisco: p. 125.

Time Pix/Gordon Parks: p. 187.

Courtesy Touro Synagogue, Newport, p. 48.

UNITE Archives, Kheel Center, Cornell University; p. 166.

Courtesy The Utah State Historical Society, Frontier Reminiscences of Eveline Brooks Auerback: p. 126 (right quilt).

Courtesy The UT Institute of Texan Cultures, San Antonio: pp. 68, 69, 76, 106, 131 (right) (Courtesy of Archives Temple B'nai Israel).

Malcolm Varon: pp. 93.

Mss SCUA University of Washington Libraries, Seattle: pp. 119, 120-121.

Courtesy Western Jewish History Center, Judah L. Magnes Museum: pp. 78 (Lipman Harris Family Collection), 79 (below) (Sophie Gerstle Lilienthal Collection), 126 (Fanny Jaffe Sharlip Collection), 134 (Florence Prag Kahn Collection).

Courtesy of Ellin Yassky: p. 231 (below).

YIVO Institute for Jewish Research: pp. 66, 126 (top photos, left quilt) (left: PO 1240-01) (right: PO 1240-01), 144-145.